The Journal Writer's Handbook

JULIET PLATT

D1501663

Contents

Thanks to my workshop participants and coaching clients who generously shared their journal writing insights. You made this book possible.

I am grateful to Julia McCutchen for her advice and guidance; and to the artistic talents of David Thelwell who provided the artwork and illustrations.

And as ever thanks to my very own 'technical monkey'. You know who you are. xx

"The moment you begin to write... you are making a declaration of independence, determining to think for yourself, to leave a record of the person you actually are, as against the person that other people would like you to be."

Dermot Bolger
Irish Times
20th August 2009

Preface

The aim of The Journal Writer's Handbook is to encourage you to pick up your pen and develop your own reflective writing practice in the form of journaling.

You might be interested in doing this as a new kind of hobby, or to nurture the writer within you to identify and develop your creative ideas. You might want to delve into the story of your life, to capture memories and significant moments that you'd like others to know about after you're gone. Or you might be interested in your own personal growth and development, in discovering new, useful and surprising things about who you are.

All these are perfectly good reasons for referring to The Journal Writer's Handbook, and I welcome you to these pages.

However there are other reasons, more far-reaching perhaps, for self-reflection in writing.

Individually and collectively we need to draw on our inner reserves of resilience, resourcefulness and creativity in order to cope with the ecological and ideological risks and threats that face us. We can't change things single-handedly, but we can ensure that as individuals we behave with integrity. Picking up a pen and making meaningful words appear on a page is the first step in taking a more reflective and considered approach to our existence. And it is no less than a miracle of cerebral re-integration, enabling the creative, emotional and intuitive part of our brain to balance with the part that is more logical, analytical and narrowly focused. By promoting this healing process, this *becoming* whole, for ourselves, we trigger a domino effect collectively.

Imagine a world where we all paid attention to getting to know ourselves and our purpose better; to tapping into our internal reservoirs of intuition and right-thinking; and to clarifying our personal responsibility, our unique contribution, and how we conduct ourselves in relation to each other, our communities and our environment. In this sense self-reflection is not self-indulgence, nor is scribbling in a notebook a mere distraction. Our writing enables us to recognise and own who we are, and this in turn allows us to act with greater purpose and integrity in our relationships and our communities.

Everything is connected. Whilst we need a wholesale reassessment of global resources in order to guarantee a sustainable future, we also need to take stock of our own motivations and intentions. Authentic reflective journal writing is one way to raise our consciousness for the sake of clear thinking and purposeful action. Simply put, by reflecting on our own thoughts and behaviour we can act more responsibly for the sake of others and our planet.

The Journal Writer's Handbook is a call for everyone to stop and reflect. Whether we consider ourselves writers or not, we should regularly take a few moments out of our lives to write down our thoughts and to think about our circumstances. We could then assess how we feel about everything that's going on around us, in our home, neighbourhood, country and world. It is a healthy way of engaging with, and applying ourselves to, reality.

We can't change the world on our own. But we can become clearer about our role in it, big or small. Journal writing enables us to find our own voice. It helps us make fulfilling choices and create our own meaning, such that the contribution we feel able to make is in service of the greatest good.

The astounding benefits of journal writing

Journal writing is recommended in many therapeutic and educational contexts, as a way of working through difficult emotions, or developing critical thinking skills by reflecting on the process of learning. However, reflective writing needn't just apply in these contexts alone. My main motivation for putting this book together is to encourage more people to experience the benefits of activating and deepening our conscious awareness through reflective writing practice.

To whet your appetite, rest assured that regular reflection in our journals helps us in everyday life to:

- Record and remember facts, figures, positive experiences, things we need to do
- Let go, de-clutter our mind and gain perspective
- See and understand more, quicker – achieving more clarity in minutes than it may have taken years already to acquire
- Concentrate and become less distracted
- Expand our mental space and our relationship with time
- Find satisfaction and fulfilment in creativity – no matter how "creative" you consider yourself to be
- Balance the different hemispheres of our brain
- Restore a sense of integration and wholeness
- Know ourselves – become familiar with our own authentic voice and thread of integrity
- Find answers to our biggest questions
- Heal ourselves

- Sleep better
- Lose weight
- Manage our physical symptoms holistically
- Identify our next steps – those that are easy *and yet* will also take us the furthest
- Carve out a meaningful role for ourselves in our surrounding community

How to use this book

My intention with the Journal Writer's Handbook is for it to provide its readers with journal writing guidance and inspiration, whether you're new to this past-time, or whether you're a seasoned journal writer, with the occasional need for a new exercise or way of tackling particular issues and situations.

With this in mind, there are various ways to "slice the cake":

- The chapters represent a curriculum of how to embark on and develop a journal writing practice, deepening the whistle-stop tour of techniques that I introduce during my day-long journaling workshops.

- With its carefully indexed exercises this is an ideal reference manual to keep handy for whenever you need a bit of journal writing inspiration.

- Also, each chapter is cross-referenced to suit different points on life's journey, so you can quickly find exercises that will help with different challenges and scenarios.

- The Mood Index appendix can be dipped into for reference when you have a particular tough mood to crack, or when you want to prolong and savour the good mood you're experiencing.

An important thing to point out is that none of what is written in this book is prescriptive. There is absolutely no right and wrong, and my greatest hope is that the exercises will lead you towards your own writing approach. And it would be great to hear what your ideas are if you'd care to share!

I invite you now to join your own personal voyage to your inner wisdom. Weigh anchor and launch yourself onto an ocean of discovery. Get to know yourself and your crew, set your course and log your journey as consciously as possible. Dive into the limpid depths of your intuitive senses and your sub-conscious mind, returning with pearls of insight. Draw on your inner strength to sit out the doldrums or face the stormy seas, but most of all stay awake on your watch, to reflect and benefit from all that you are learning, to make your voyage as fulfilling and purposeful as possible.

Bon Voyage!

"The meaning of your life is the meaning you give it; it consists in what you create through the identification and pursuit of endeavours that your talents fit you for and your interests draw you to."

A C Grayling

Chapter 1

Weighing anchor

To take up your journal is to begin a new journey of discovery. As the captain of your journaling ship you will want to get to know your vessel and all who set sail in her. You may venture into uncharted territory, and encounter inclement conditions, but you can be safe in the knowledge that your journaling vessel is completely sea-worthy and that its crew has unparalleled experience and wisdom in these waters.

The anchor is weighed and you are on your way.

What to write in?

Your choice of journal is entirely personal to you. It really doesn't matter if you buy a job lot of school exercise books from the supermarket or spend luxurious time browsing for that perfect, beautiful, leather-bound journal. You might equally choose a box of biros or a perfectly crafted gold-nibbed ink-pen to write with as well. The act of writing your journal can be as functional and utilitarian or as sensuous as you choose. I've taken both approaches in the past – panic-buying a notebook and cheap pen at the airport having realised a need to write *right now*, and not having brought along anything fit for the purpose; or spending ages salivating over pristine leather bound pages in a range of tantalising jacket covers, trying to determine which one fits the season and how it resonates with my writing intentions.

These days I choose to have an attractive but inexpensive notebook on hand at all times. I choose it carefully, but don't pay the earth for it, so I simultaneously satisfy my sensuous requirement and my occasional need to scribble untidily without a sense of defacement.

There are numerous 'journals on a theme' available, such as book journals, travel journals, wine journals, gardening journals. If it helps to get started on writing around a particular interest or hobby then these are very useful, and will add another dimension to your leisure time. They can become reflective documents as much as records of events if you take the time to write about how the book, journey, bottle of wine or plant made you feel, what it awakened in you and what it added to your life experience. Similarly you might choose your own journal theme, such as gratitude, happiness or success, and dedicate it to reflecting on each of these experiences.

So the choice is yours. The only thing I would stipulate is that you do actually choose to write with a pen directly onto the page. This blending of fine motor skill with the production of meaningful words is important in delivering the cerebrally integrating benefits of writing. It also encourages truth and authenticity in contrast with typing on a keyboard, which may encourage us to write in persona, to be other than we are or to be less honest about ourselves.

How often?

There are no rules about how often you write. Some people write every day, others whenever the mood takes them, others when they are in desperate need of a writing fix, when they approach each page with the feverishness and urgency of a chain-smoker.

"I was really good at the beginning of the year," said one full-time Mum and aspiring novelist at one of my journal writing workshops. "I filled in my diary every day for a couple of weeks, but then life got in the way and the next time I got back to it was about six months later, when I felt it would be a bit of a waste of time to start again."

To avoid the situation of having blank days, I choose not to have pre-printed dates in my journal. I use a non-lined notebook, with smooth paper that doesn't blotch my ink, and I write in the date myself. This way it doesn't matter how often I pick up my pen to write. There are often weeks, months and sometimes years between entries.

Get writing!

At first, having acquired your notebook, you may feel hesitant about making a mark on it. You don't want to spoil it; doubt that you have anything meaningful to say; are worried about how well you write, spell and use punctuation. My response to all of these wriggly excuses is just do it! Think of your brand new journal as an empty chest, as only a fraction of what it could be if it was filled with your words. Only then can it become a real treasure.

And remember your journal is a private document. There are no rules here, except the constraints that you are setting for yourself. Many of those you're probably going to want to get over – so you may as well start straight away.

In my journal writing workshops I make it very clear that participants are under no obligation to share anything they write, though sometimes people become so excited by the insights they are discovering, that they cannot help but share.

Occasionally participants say it's hard to get going and to know how to make a start. One lady even asked whether it would be possible for me to go home with her and be on hand to tell her to sit and write, and give her an opening phrase to get her writing. Left to her own devices, she said she would probably find a phone call she needed to make or a cake she had to bake instead. Hopefully by having this book to hand as you make time to write you won't be short of ideas for long.

The key is to stay curious, keep writing, and to trust the words that appear at the end of the pen without trying to censor or manipulate them too much. This is a good exercise in letting go and giving our minds a rest.

So on the first page – or wherever you choose to begin (no rules see) - I recommend you write today's date. It is useful when reflecting on your progress to know on which date you wrote. Life needs a certain chronology; but this doesn't mean to say we need to be bound and gagged by time. Acknowledging time and respecting it for no more than it is - a date marker in this instance – means that our relationship with it in the long run will be a lot easier and healthier.

Eventually, as you become more adept and comfortable with writing in your journal, you may want to let go of having to explain context and circumstances in great detail. This is not a document to give anyone else insight into your life. It's about giving *you* more insight into a life you know because you are living it. So instead of beginning a rainy day entry describing the laborious process of finding your raincoat and your umbrella, why not begin it succinctly with "Rain today." Then go on to reflect on *why* it took so long to find the things you needed! Or, having found your brolly, you might reflect on its story - where you acquired it, how long ago, what it means to you, and what memories it evokes. This is reflective writing as opposed to event recording, and it is much more enjoyable, sustainable and rewarding.

The important point here is not to make journal writing a chore. As soon as it begins to feel like an obligation to sit and write, and fill your nice page-per-day lockable five-year-diary with neat recordings of every day's events, you're likely to be fighting a lost cause. You will quickly get bored and lose momentum. Like ripe fruit, the nutritious juice in journal writing is to be found under the surface of daily events - not in the events themselves.

What does your journal mean to you?
How you relate to your journal – and therefore how you begin to write in it – is entirely up to you. Of course to get going you may choose initially to use your journal simply as a notebook to record, make lists and write down goals. There is nothing wrong with this, and you will very quickly experience the benefits of having a clearer mind and greater focus on the tasks in hand, with an increased capacity to resist distractions.

You will also begin to notice an expansion of time, and an ability to get more done more quickly as you develop an appreciation of how long it really takes to accomplish a task. Writing things down helps us to strip away all the anxiety and procrastination from the things we need to do and enables us to see tasks for what they are.

You may choose to use your journal only in conjunction with a particular project or programme you're working on. This can be anything from installing a new bathroom to attending a course of spiritual awakening. Having intentions, commitments, focus, resourcefulness, resolve, and the ability to celebrate achievements, is as important in one activity as in the other, and our journals facilitate the process of reflective learning from each aspect.

Many journal writers have addressed their words *to* their journal, as if it is a friend or third person in its own right. Anne Frank addressed her journal entries to Kitty, relating to her journal as her closest friend, to help her achieve a deep sense of comfort during unutterably terrifying and tragic times. On a symbolic level Kitty actually represents Anne's own inner resilience to deal with the deeply traumatic events that were surrounding her life. This inner resourcefulness is available to all of us, and journal writing is the perfect way to access it.

Similarly, Elizabeth Gilbert, author of the acclaimed best seller Eat Pray Love, turned to her journal as her absolute final refuge when life felt too grim and she was struggling to find her way forward. She describes speaking in her notebook to her potential self, the person she is becoming, whose wisdom and guidance are the salvation of the person she is being right now, the one needing help. At first this still small voice came to her in answer to a prayer, and she mistook it for the voice of God. Eventually however she realised that this was her own voice, infinitely present and accessible to her through her journal, her authentic voice of common sense, wisdom and truth.

Relating to your journal as an intelligent entity in its own right invites another voice into the equation. It also facilitates the process of getting out of our own way so that we can allow for new perspectives. There are a number of exercises, such as *Writing as, RSVP* and *Communing*, to facilitate this practice of shifting point of view, which ultimately serves to deepen our self-awareness and enables us to let go of our judgments about other people and situations.

It is traditional, when meeting somebody for the first time, to introduce ourselves. So you may like to begin your first journal entry with an introduction. You may wish to include a greeting - Dear Diary or simply Hello. You may then want to say who you are, your name or what you believe, depending on the depth you want to go to. Then write a pen portrait of yourself. Remember the blurb we used to have to write when introducing ourselves to our first pen friend: what we like to do, what gets up our nose, our favourite curry, rock band, book, film, the colour of our bedroom wall-paper – anything goes to serve as a kick-off to introducing ourselves.

Exercise 1 – Kick off phrases
Using any of the following phrases, embark on ten minutes of free-writing with the intention of exploring who you are, what relationships you have, what your approach and attitude to life is:

- *"I firmly believe that.."*
- *"Today I am..."*
- *"It really gets up my nose when..."*
- *"My bedroom wall-paper is..."*
- *"The first time I tasted..."*
- *"In this moment..."*

Kick-off phrases such as these will become very useful tools in creating your reflective writing practice. They are a fun and stimulating way to open your journaling session. You may begin to collect them for yourself, or have a number of favourite ones up your sleeve that never fail to get you writing.

If, as you write in response to these kick-off phrases, you experience any insights, you may choose to incorporate them into your writing as well. Maybe your observations about the colour of your bedroom wall-paper are causing you to get curious about the lack of calm in your life, or the way you always allow your partner to dictate on matters of interior décor – and what *that* might be about.

This is an example of how quickly we can awaken our perceptions and understanding about what might really be going on under the surface of our life. If we just stop to notice and take some time to reflect we can very quickly get to a point of shift in our realisations.

By the bottom of your first page, what is it that you will have discovered about you? What is more, having had an insight based on your wall-paper musings, you may already be sensing some action arising from it that you wish to take straightaway.

Redecorate perhaps. Actively seek and create opportunities for a greater sense of calm in your life. Or renegotiate with your partner how you can reclaim some space that is uniquely yours in your home.

No later than the end of the second page of your journal you may already have achieved fifteen minutes of creative entertainment, a new insight into your life and experience, and new ideas about how to move forward to bring these things more in line with who you uniquely are. You may already be on the path to a more fulfilling and authentic life. In fifteen minutes - doesn't it feel good to be obtaining some mastery over time?

Exercise 2 – Getting present
Wherever you are sitting to do your writing take a moment to look around.

- *What are you noticing? Use all your senses to become aware of your environment – hearing, smell, touch, and sight – even taste!*
- *What are you aware of in your body? Is there any tension? What temperature is it?*
- *What's the energy like around you? What's your own energy level?*

Take a moment to describe in your journal the first thing that captures your attention, or the thing that you cannot ignore. How does what you are describing reflect your state of mind? What messages are you garnering from your environment to guide your inquiry and learning?

Journal writer's story

HR professional, coach and full-time working Mum Gwen used this exercise to get curious about the contents of her bathroom cabinet. Her particular self-coaching style comes across very powerfully. Here's what she found herself writing:

"Who uses the bathroom cabinet?

Me and my husband

What does it look like?

It is a 3 door oak faced cabinet, 2-3m wide, with two sinks on top (one for him and one for me).

What else can I see?

He has a small number of items stacked neatly on the left side of his sink – and the rest of the surface is taken up by my junk!

Junk?

Yes – that's what it looks like. I have a wooden tray piled high with tubes of cream, brushes, cotton buds/wool, contact lenses – and FIVE (!!??) different deodorants. Ok – so it's not "junk" – but I do have a lot of different products.....and I want to clarify that I don't have a personal hygiene problem!

What do I like about his side of the cabinet?

Well for a start, it's easier to clean around! But, apart from this, I like the simplicity – he has settled on a small number of items that do the job they're designed for. I'm slightly envious that he doesn't have all the clutter....but...

How do I really feel about this?
I can't help but feel that his side of the sink looks rather boring. Perhaps that's not the right word.................

What does "boring" mean to me?
I think I mean that there is no variety. Yes, the products are functional – but I'm not sure I like the idea of using the same ones every day. Let's face it, personal care isn't exactly stimulating – and anything that makes it a more interesting process has got to be a plus.

Speak more about "variety"...
I guess it isn't just about making things more interesting. I'm struggling to put my finger on this – but I do wonder whether the variety of products on my bathroom cabinet has something to do with striving for something ideal or perfect. However, in my search to find the ideal product I have created a huge amount of clutter – as I constantly discard the products that I already have.

Rather strangely, I am starting to wonder whether my bathroom cabinet is a powerful metaphor for the way I behave in other aspects of my life....... and whether there is something to be said for finding the right products and sticking with them.......or is that boring?

Say more.......

Well I've always had high standards - and I think constantly striving to be something better, someone better leads me to be overly critical of myself. Self-criticism gets in my way and prevents me from enjoying who I am and what I have right now – prevents me from enjoying the present.

When do these high standards get in my way?

It's an everyday thing. "I'm not good at this", "not as good as X at that" - it's just mind chatter – but the pressure I put myself under can be overwhelming.

So, what can I learn from my bathroom cabinet?

This all sounds rather improbable – but what if the clutter in my bathroom cabinet is symptomatic of a trait that infiltrates other aspects of my life? Perhaps I'm searching for the ideal product – without stopping to think that the ones I have already will do the job! I have certainly identified a "self-critical" gremlin that needs to be flushed down the bathroom toilet.

I guess I have also proven that clarity can come from the most unusual places. It's definitely time to clean out the bathroom cabinet, get rid of the junk, flush the gremlin down the toilet and identify the core products that serve me well.......

And – what's BORING about that????"

Exercise 3 – Writing as...

As you get to know your journaling vessel, you might want to know who else you have on board. Does your journal have a voice and character of its own?

As you write, who are you imagining is your audience? Is it a friend, a guide, or, like Elizabeth Gilbert, does your journal represent your potential self?

Take a moment to write back to yourself as if you are your journal.

- What does your journal have to say to you?
- What is the message it has for you today as you begin your exploration?

Chapter 2

Setting the course

Journaling is an ideal tool to accompany a life-changing plan and to help us achieve certain goals. Whether this is studying for A levels in preparation for university, devising a career change, or even learning new techniques in playing your favourite sport, knowing where you've come from, where you're heading, and what life will be like when you get there are all vital elements of planning your journey.

Where you've come from

It is useful to reflect on our past as we set our future course, and to see the kinds of things we gravitated towards as a young person, or even as a child. Our natural gifts, talents and abilities are often much easier to see in the context of our young life, before we were too much influenced and conditioned by our education, our peers or the media. Rediscovering something we used to enjoy in our youth and rekindling the practice in our current life can have the effect of reconnecting us with our youthful intentions, hopes and dreams. Many of these may have been lost in the mists of time, forgotten about or dismissed as naïve fantasies as we have forged our path in the grown-up world.

However, when we feel bored or exhausted with life in middle age, calling to mind the things we loved to do as children and then making room for them once more, can have a very powerful effect in waking us up to new possibilities for ourselves.

At the age of 38 I rediscovered the joy of cycling. As a young child my bike was my playmate and I would spend hours cycling around my local neighbourhood. These days I try and use my bike instead of taking the car and I find it never fails to cheer me up. It's also a great trigger of creative ideas, and although it's not exactly conducive to note-taking, sometimes it's good just to let the imagination run.

Taking a mental journey back to our childhood to remember favourite objects, places, events and people can also provide us with rich journaling material, as well as inform us about what's needed in our present experience to move us forward. Once again, our relationship with time shifts in our journals as we are able to condense past and future into this present moment in our writing.

During his visit to Desert Island Discs on BBC Radio 4, singer songwriter Barry Manilow declared that a privileged life was one in which you made a career out of what you loved to do at thirteen. For him that was composing music. It's fascinating and insightful to inquire what that might look like in our own lives.

Exercise 4 – Back in time
Spend a few minutes writing in response to the following kick-off phrase:

- *"When I was 13 I used to love…"*

*If 13 is an age you'd rather forget, choose a different age, the one you feel has the richest message in it for you now. Allow your mind to drift to that time in your childhood, and watch the **thought-movie** of how your life used to be.*

- *What activities do you remember engaging in the most?*
- *What were your favourite clothes to wear?*
- *What made you laugh?*
- *What did you most look forward to?*
- *What would your current life be like if you reintroduced some of these childhood pastimes?*

Where you're heading
Goal-setting is traditionally recommended as an ideal tool to begin to shape the future and get an idea about what it is possible for us to create in our lives.

However I perceive a significant problem with the concept of goal-setting which is often the reason why people fail to reach their goals, or repeatedly shift the goal posts before finally giving up altogether.

During my journaling workshops, I invite participants to stand up, close their eyes, and bring to mind a goal that they would like to achieve in their lives. I then ask them to point to the goal.

In fifty per cent of cases people will point away from themselves, typically in front of themselves, to a goal which exists outside them, at an indeterminate distance, beyond a number of obstacles, barriers to overcome and "if-onlys" to be satisfied. They are already aware of the hard work and determination they are going to need to achieve the goal they have in mind. Some of them know that they will apply themselves as assiduously as they need to in order to get there, and will already have specific action plans in place and a clear schedule of what needs to be done to get them from where they are now to where they want to be.

Many of them will have a sneaky, niggling feeling that this goal is unrealistic, and they will already be preparing their excuses for not achieving it. When a goal feels out of reach to begin with, because we perceive it to be outside ourselves, it is extremely difficult to persuade ourselves that we will ever finally get there. With this mindset, the failure rate can be quite high.

By way of contrast, in the other fifty per cent of cases people will find they are pointing to their head, their feet or their heart. This is very encouraging, and it illustrates an important point about the goals we set for ourselves.

Rather than trying to reach for something that is outside of us, at a different point in space and time from where we are, we can conceive of goals as intentions we carry with us at all times. Our intentions are borne out of our already existing experiences, desires and motivations, and they become real when we give them a name and regularly practise reflecting on them.

Journal writer's story

Lavinia wanted to write her first novel. Through journaling she became aware that by setting herself a very clear intention to become a novelist, and by committing herself to regularly practising the skills, talents and gifts she already had within herself, her goal became very real, close and achievable. Here's what she wrote:

"It was all very well setting myself a goal to write a book for publication, and visualising the end product. But I knew the only way I can legitimately call myself a writer is by actually getting on and doing some writing. Writing is a skill I've had all my life, so bringing this together with my natural ability to observe others, and my gift for story-telling, there is really nothing to stop me from writing right now and moving towards my goal."

I do not wish to dismiss goal-setting entirely. It's useful and motivating to have something to aim for; however the focus doesn't need to be constantly on what's outside, or what's in the future. Much more helpful is to know more about what our life experience has already equipped us with, and what intentions we already carry within us for the life we are creating. The building blocks of future possibilities already lie within our hands. Developing an ability to distinguish between the things that motivate us and the things we can readily apply ourselves to straight away is a useful way to understand and put into practice our current level of inner resourcefulness. (And this I guarantee is far greater already than we give ourselves credit for.)

Don't forget to take a map!
Consider the following equation:

Ability + Motivation + Action = Potential.

These things taken as a whole provide us with A MAP of our ideal navigation course. In journaling parlance, I think of Ability as being the whole host of skills, talents and gifts we already have at our disposal. Motivation equates to the interests and values that we hold, and Action is what we commit to doing on a regular basis to give expression to our abilities. Once all these things are in alignment, and, crucially, feel authentic to us, then we have the best chance of reaching our true Potential.

Take a moment to draw a circle, split into four quadrants:

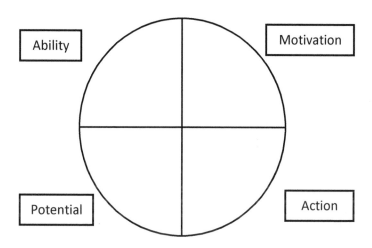

Each quadrant represents one of Ability, Motivation, Action and Potential.

Taking the centre of the circle to be 0 and the outer edge of each quadrant to be 10, draw a new circumference line within each quadrant indicating on a scale of 0-10 your current level of understanding of each of the elements.

If you're full of action, but are not so clear on your innate abilities or values, the likelihood is you're not reaching your full potential, and the wheel might look a bit like this:

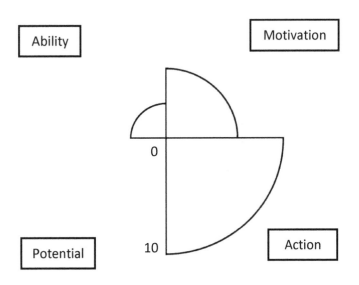

Not only is part of it missing altogether, the other quadrants would make it a very bumpy ride indeed, and the bike would be extremely hard to pedal!

We can use our journals to focus on and achieve clarity about each of these elements, so that we can create a wheel which runs a lot more smoothly, and which facilitates a much easier ride to achieve our full potential.

To identify the things that we are naturally gifted at, in which we have an innate interest, and those things to which we commit ourselves, the classic journaling tool of list-writing comes into its own.

Exercise 5 – Lists of Distinction

This is an exercise that is in three parts. You'll need at least forty minutes to work through all of it in one go, or you might choose to split it down and work on it in shorter journaling sessions. At the end of it you will have five separate lists, enabling you to draw distinctions between some of your abilities, motivations and actions. It is useful to get clear on these concepts and what they mean to us, thus avoiding the temptation of collapsing them together into the stuff of our life, where they become invisible and unusable.

To begin with, spend a couple of minutes on each of the following 3 distinct lists, under the headings:

- *My Skills*
- *My Talents*
- *My Gifts*

These represent your Abilities, either that you have learned or that you naturally possess. As a way of distinguishing them further I am choosing to designate our gifts as those natural abilities that we happily share for the benefit of others. But don't get too hung up on this if it's tricky to differentiate. The benefit of this exercise lies in the process of recognising that we have a number of distinct abilities: the semantics are less important.

For example: driving a car is a skill I have learned; being able to touch the tip of my nose with my tongue is one of my talents; and my ability to provide a safe environment for people to learn about themselves is my gift.

Next, write a list of bullet-points in response to the following kick-off phrase: "I am interested in...".

This list will contain the things that catch your attention, and that you are naturally motivated to find out about. These are the things that you will stop to read about in a newspaper or magazine, or that you will tune in specially to watch on TV.

Finally write a list in response to the following kick-off phrase: "I am committed to..."

In this list you will note all the things that you currently have a real commitment to doing, and which you are regularly fulfilling by taking action. It may be tempting to note down more idealistic things here, such as 'I am committed to caring for the environment', but unless you are actively and consciously out there taking action, picking up litter, recycling, using less fossil fuel etc. these commitments are little more than pipe-dreams. Get real – your journal is not the place to kid yourself.

For example: A real commitment for me would be ensuring that my family and I sit down together and share a home-cooked meal 3 – 4 times a week.

Exercise 6 – Values inquiry
Our values are like the pedal power that pushes our bike along. They are the things that make our life tick over in a unique way. They are what we look for, what are important to us, and what we find life difficult without. They show us the reason behind our actions and our motivations, and shed new light on our potential when combined with our abilities.

Reflecting on the lists of distinction you have created, choose one of your commitments and pose yourself the following inquiry:

- *"What's important to me about...? (Sharing a home-cooked meal with my family)"*

Take a few minutes to consider this and to respond to it in your journal. Pay attention to the words and phrases that come up for you.

In my example, I would find that ideas such as nutrition, conversation, togetherness, and health would come up. So drilling a little bit further into these and finding out what's so important about them, I would find the value of loving the family unit sitting right at the heart of my weekly commitment.

I love my kids, and I love hearing their thoughts and opinions. I want them to be healthy and feel secure enough to express themselves: sharing a home-cooked meal and conversation a few days a week is important to me in ensuring these things.

Exercise 7 – Mix n' match
Remember that children's game where you put different tops, middles and bottoms of pictures together in a funny order? I used to like the one of the policeman wearing a clown's dungarees and sporting a mermaid's tail.

Take one item from each of your lists of distinction and your values inquiry and put them together to form a new intention. You might even make yourself a set of differently coded cards which you can shuffle and draw to give you new inspiration.

For example: I am interested in the outdoor life. I can ride a bike and I am committed to doing my bit for the environment. The intention I'm setting is to use my bike whenever possible instead of taking the car.

Or: Honesty is important to me. I am good with words and I can use a computer. I have the gift of curiosity and of being able to get people to relax and open up. The intention I'm setting is to find work as an ethical journalistic reporter.

Now set your goal – and fulfil your potential

Once we have defined our intentions the next logical step is to set ourselves a goal. Such as: building on my intention to use my bike more regularly my goal is to lose five kilos in three months. Or: following my intention to work in journalism my goal is to submit a feature for publication next month.

Thus our goals are built on the intentions that we are setting ourselves from within, from our abilities, motivations and actions. Having a clear and distinct understanding of all of these elements gives us the ability to combine them in fresh ways, and create potentially achievable goals.

Exercise 8 – Letter from the future

Identify a date in the future by when you will have put your intentions into practice and achieved your goals.

Write the date down, and then begin to write a letter back to your present-day self from that date in the future.

Consider the following questions:

- *What is life like?*
- *What does your day consist of?*
- *What are the sights, sounds and smells of life in the future?*
- *Where are you writing from?*

- *What will you be doing after you've finished this letter?*
- *What special message do you have for your present day self? What encouragements can your future self give?*

Chapter 3

Logging the Journey

It is the responsibility of the ship's captain to keep a careful log of weather conditions, the time it takes to cover certain distances, and what's happening on board. As the captain of the ship of your life your journal represents your ship's log. You can note down not just what the climatic reality is, but what you see en route and how your ship is behaving. Observational skills and a heightened awareness of what is happening in the present moment are vital to retain control of the vessel, avert danger, and respond quickly and efficiently in an emergency.

Far from being a fantastical distraction or self-indulgent ego-trip, reflective writing helps us stay honest, grounded and present to the reality of our experience. Using our journals to pay particular attention to what's going on in both our external and internal environment, as well as deepening our awareness of our individual rhythm and preferred routines, we can help ourselves become better prepared for whatever the journey throws at us.

The benefits of getting present
To develop a sense of presence means becoming aware of ourselves and our surroundings, right now. It means being available, able to sense and respond to whatever we see, hear, smell, taste, touch and feel from one moment to the next. It also means being able to calm down the continuous future and past obsessed voice in our heads. The voice which is constantly running a commentary on what we've done, why we've done it, what other people might think about what we've done and what we're going to do next. Of course each of these commentary headlines run their own extensive sub-plots and what-ifs. So we need never run out of material which takes us right out of the present moment to be elsewhere, lost in our imaginations and thoughts. Meanwhile the benefits of developing an awareness of the present moment are considerable, not least because we completely transform our relationship to time by living in, and using up, every single moment.

A couple of years ago I took a brand new journal on holiday with me. I was all set to enjoy a quiet break in the sun, with nothing to do except savour whatever was happening in the moment. With clean, crisp pages available to me on which to record the things I noticed I had an amazing holiday. Each day I spent a little bit of time writing and reflecting. I wrote about where I was staying, what I saw, how I reacted, and the people I met. I tried to put into words the feeling of sun on my skin, the beauty of the light in my room during my afternoon siesta, the effect of the music from my mp3 player. I reflected on the relationships in my life, on what I was learning about myself and others. It was a very rich week, though it felt like much longer, possibly because I wrote and reflected on so much during that time. It felt as if I was living each moment twice.

From this experience I learned a number of things. Firstly, that there is an economical benefit to journaling about our present experience. It means we can buy shorter, less expensive holidays and get double the value from them by being aware of and savouring each moment! Then, having written all about it in our journal, we are free to relive moments of that holiday for ever after!

The second thing I learned was how not being in the present cheats us of time, and gives us a warped perception of *'the time things take'* .How many times do we cheat ourselves of our last day on holiday because we pack the evening before, and by the time we wake up in the morning we find we've already left? Energetically we're already on the plane home, even though we still might have eight hours before the bus arrives to take us to the airport.

And it pays to be aware of our inner commentator's view of everyday chores. Even though it only takes two and a half minutes for me to sort the laundry into colour piles, load each pile, put in the detergent and switch on the machine, my inner commentator has managed to convince me that this is a job that takes ages. Unsorted piles of dirty clothes sit on the floor for days, until I have a sufficiently lengthy window of time to sort them.

Likewise, it takes ten minutes to put clean washing away. Yet I typically have basket upon basket of clean clothes sitting around gathering dust for days before I'll do anything about them. Thanks to my inner commentator, I have developed the perception, entirely reinforced by my desultory habits in this regard, that it takes a whole week to do the washing, even though each load takes a maximum of two to three hours from colour sorting through to putting away.

Conversely, using our journal to develop a sense of what it is to be present quickly shows us that it doesn't really take very long to pack a suitcase or do our chores. In fact, it's our level of anxiety about the activity, our constant mind chatter and inner commentary before, during and after, which makes 'the time things take' expand in our consciousness. As a result we develop time-wasting habits, continually allowing for more time than we actually need to carry out an activity. But we can avoid being derailed by our inner commentator. Tuning in to our honest inner voice through reflective writing allows us to have a calmer perspective on our present reality, and make the most of each moment.

Exercise 9 – Sensory survey
Take a moment to tune in to the sights, sounds and smells of your journal writing environment.

- *What do you hear?*
- *What can you smell?*
- *What is the quality of the light?*
- *What is the feeling of the pen in your fingers? What is the ambient temperature?*
- *How comfortably are you sitting?*
- *How does your seat feel beneath you?*
- *What are you aware of in your body?*
- *If there is anything trying to tug you away from this exercise – a thought or anxiety about something – what is it?*
- *What are your senses getting ready for next?*

Exercise 10 – Pen Portraits

Bring to mind an individual who has had a particular impact on you over the past week. This person may be real, fictional, alive or dead, local to you or someone you have seen or heard on television or radio.

Write a portrait of them.

- *What are their physical features?*
- *What are they wearing?*
- *What are they carrying?*
- *What are they doing?*
- *How do they speak?*
- *What do they say?*
- *How do they affect you?*
- *What question do you have for them?*
- *And what is their answer?*

What's your rhythm?

As a working mum the needs and demands of those around me occupy a large chunk of my time, and can often feel overwhelming. What is more, mums are very much the barometer of the whole household, and what we sometimes notice is that if we're out of sorts, so is everyone else at home. Sometimes, this can feel like a huge responsibility, and can even feel quite oppressive.

On the other hand it emphasises the importance of being able to do things our own way, according to our own pace, and without the extra pressure of trying to live up to anyone else's expectations.

So paying attention to our natural rhythm and preferred routine is an important step in establishing how to enhance our present experience and live authentically.

Whether you're a morning person or a night owl; whether there are certain times of the week or the month when you feel more energetic or more subdued than others - there is no wrong or right way, no matter what your inner commentator says. There is only your way.

The monthly cycle

This has been a taboo subject for too long and as women we are expected – and expect ourselves – to sail through each month regardless of what's happening to us physiologically, mentally and emotionally.

Yet these expectations are nonsensical, particularly for women who work for themselves. In our own businesses we are free to call the shots, and we no longer have to struggle on through our most difficult and exhausting days just because the business world normally dances to the beat of a male drum.

There is nothing stopping us from paying close attention to how our hormonal cycle affects us each month, and responding to the rhythm in whatever way seems right and most effective for us at the time.

As a broad brush generalisation we tend to be more out-going, chatty, self-confident, energetic, able to focus and multi-task in the first two weeks of our cycle, from the first day of our period, when oestrogen and testosterone are on the rise. For me this is certainly the time when I'm more able to think on my feet, have some great ideas, and turn lots of things round very quickly. Knowing this about how I am has meant these weeks can be the most productive in my business – the best times for networking, pitching, making presentations, doing talks and leading workshops.

By the start of week three the effect of rising progesterone can be felt, which makes us calmer, more reflective, introverted, and possibly prone to day-dreaming. This might also be a time when we become a bit emotional, and are more likely to take things personally. It's a good time to get stuck into some admin, or review your business plan, or get on with a focused task that has a deadline looming. It might also be a time to let our imagination run wild and write down lots of creative ideas for where our enterprise might go next.

By week four oestrogen and testosterone are plummeting. Confidence levels are at their lowest, so perhaps this isn't the time for innovation and expansion. Typically this is a time when we need to be kindest to ourselves, not putting on any extra pressure, and if we want to take the phone off the hook, put our feet up and eat lots of chocolate then so be it. It's your business; you are completely free to do it your way.

Of course sometimes it will be impossible to dictate events all the time according to our cycle. However, by knowing exactly where we are in our cycle, how our fluctuating hormones affect us and what we can reasonably expect from ourselves, it is much easier to plan ahead and prepare as much as possible.

Exercise 11 – A life in a day/week/month
Put some time aside each day to pay attention to your activities, moods and energy levels and to log them in your journal. Our sleep patterns, digestive system, growth cycles, periods and dreams are all rhythmic processes. Pay attention to them and make a note of what you become aware of.

If you have some physical symptoms, make a commitment to log these too on a daily basis.

- *What's possible for you at different times?*
- *What's easy or more difficult?*

- *What role does your mood or energy level play?*
- *What happens to your symptoms as you pay attention to them?*
- *What commitments is it time to cull?*
- *What new things would you like to make room for?*

Over the week or month you will begin to get a picture of your natural rhythm and routine, and reflect on whether you are honouring it or trying to go at a pace that isn't your own.

Making use of what you notice

Using our journals to write descriptive passages of where we are and whom we meet is a rewarding way to enhance our present awareness and make our experience timeless. However, this does little more than put our experience into words. It doesn't necessarily deepen our insight and understanding.

We can go further on our reflective journey, and make greater use of what we notice. The use of metaphor is a vital tool to help us in this quest. It also encourages great cerebral integration, as what our left brain has put into words our right brain can re-adopt and transform into learning.

In the context of our voyage of self-discovery, treasure is the metaphor for the knowledge, wisdom and understanding we bring back from our travels within. The Hero's Journey is a well-known metaphor for the trials and tests that call individuals forth and help them grow. Devised by American mythologist and writer Joseph Campbell, the Hero's Journey essentially comprises the stages of departure, initiation and return, with many challenges along the way, and rich learning to reintegrate into everyday life.

The whole of this journaling guide is in itself modelled on the circular journey - weighing anchor, logging the journey, diving in, riding out the storms and the doldrums and returning safely home with new riches to reflect upon. Every time we pick up our journals we have the opportunity to dive deeper and return with some new nugget of insight. Giving ourselves time to retreat and reflect on our circumstances, thoughts and emotions yields a great amount of learning and inspiration for how to move forward.

Metaphor is a useful tool for those times when we feel particularly stuck and cannot readily find the forward path for ourselves. It enables us to find fresh perspectives and impetus to try a different tack and break out of our normal thought patterns and routine responses. Using metaphor is also a way of exercising our creative muscle and forging new neural pathways. When we catch ourselves going over the same old broken record of thinking, we can choose to lift the needle, snap the vinyl and scroll down to a brand new mp3 track instead!

The dictionary definition of metaphor is:

"the application of name and descriptive term or phrase to an object or action to which it is imaginatively but not literally applicable"

In the broken record example the action of changing our old habits is metaphorically substituted by chucking out the disc and the gramophone and switching to digital music. We then find meaning for ourselves in the adjectives that describe the new approach - it's more direct, less cluttered, cleaner, and more compact. In this way we set ourselves new intentions and aspirations.

Fascinatingly, it is much simpler to go straight ahead and use metaphor than it is to describe it. We seem to have a direct ability to understand creative connections and substitutions and to draw meaning from them in terms of our own situation. This is linked to our human need for, and appreciation of, stories to guide and inform us.

Indulging in metaphor in our journals is therefore a simple exercise which requires little technical ability beyond being able to see one thing as an imaginative substitute for another.

Anything will serve as a metaphor for us to reflect on our situation. If from our sensory survey we have picked up on a bird singing we might use the sound to trigger a metaphorical exploration in our journals.

"My bird song is..." might be a useful kick-off phrase. Alternatively we could play with a conditional phrase "If I were a bird singing my way through this issue I would..."

Here's a cautionary metaphorical tale, written in response to the loud noise I could hear as I wrote, with an impassioned plea for help:

12ᵗʰ February

Living my life at the pace of a power saw I am constantly whizzing, and I go at everything I touch with pure unadulterated vigour and violence. I am relentless, slicing through everything with which I come into contact, screeching, buzzing, humming, until the two halves of my focus fall lifeless to the floor. I am a danger to live with. My

impact is devastating and my power
terrifying. Please someone pull my plug.

There are many access routes into metaphor. We can take any everyday object as our metaphorical model in the moment; we can draw on nature, animals, the seasons, established archetypes or narrative patterns such as the Hero's Journey; or we can develop our own reliable cast of characters and mythologies to support our personal explorations.

Exercise 12 – Playing with metaphors

1. Take the kick-off phrase "Today I am" and complete it with the first everyday object that comes to mind as you write.

Don't censor, keep writing, getting curious about what it is to be such an object, what your particular uses or talents are, and what you are learning.

There is no need to be very attached to the object. You do not need to fully identify yourself with it forever. Treat this is an exercise in helping you explore new possibilities and new awareness about your circumstances.

2. Remember Forrest Gump? His Ma's advice began "Life is like a box of chocolates – you never know what you're gonna get." Granted, it's more a simile than a metaphor, but you could try the kick-off phrase "Life is like" and see what your journal has to show you.

3. Try a metaphorical inquiry, which is an open question to get you thinking. For example:

- *"What's the toy inside my Kinder Egg?"*
- *"What's a new web I can weave?"*
- *"What is on each of the plates I'm spinning?"*

Time for a cargo check!

So far, with the help of your journal you may now be aware of your expanding reflective ability. You will be starting to recognise and identify some of your inner-most resources. The exercises so far have introduced you to your interests, talents, skills, gifts, intentions and commitments; the voice of your journal or your potential self; your natural rhythm and your preferred routine. You have also begun to rediscover that innate human tendency to find metaphors through which to interpret your experience.

I hope that all these tools and resources are beginning to contribute to a rich and rewarding reflective experience for you.

Chapter 4

Diving in

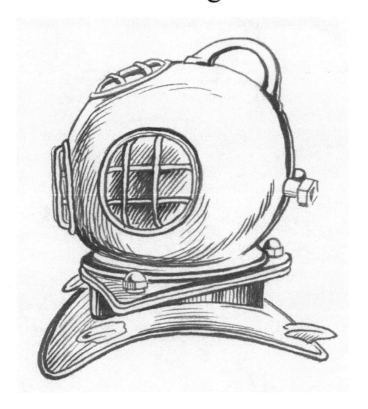

Our voyage is well underway and we have already covered a lot of nautical miles. Having worked hard there is nothing sweeter than to spend a while diving in to the warm turquoise waters of our inner powers, and allowing our bodies to enjoy just splashing about in the blue. There are many pearls of wisdom to be brought back to the surface. Taking a few moments on a regular basis to settle down with our journal and note whatever needs to be noted on the page is a simple and effective way of redressing the balance in our lives. We can salvage some calm from the cacophony of things to do, obligations to keep and inner criticisms to fend off.

The physicality of our intelligence
Intuition is another name for the intelligence of our bodies, and we typically use very physical or sensual words and phrases to refer to our intuitive hits: "gut reaction"; "hunch"; "follow your nose"; "keep your ear to the ground"; "feel it in your water or your bones"; "sniff something out"; "something doesn't smell right." Reflective writing is a great way to build up our intuitive muscles. By trusting that what appears on the page is what we most need to work with in this moment, we can begin to allow ourselves to be guided by our intuition in other areas of life.

Intuition has been given a bad press over the years. Western culture views it with suspicion and discredits its use as inferior to the cold hard analysis of irrefutable fact. There is also a myth that goes along with the successful intuition theory, that states people that must already have a degree of manifested success before intuition works properly. That is, it's OK to follow your gut instinct as long as you're not risking too much.

However the tide is beginning to turn, and even though intuitive operators have known it for years, they now find themselves supported in their convictions by the emerging understanding of neuroscience, and the role of the sub-conscious. Research shows that our intuitive responses are triggered well in advance – by a matter of seconds – of our conscious ability to process the information. We also know that our responses can usually be felt in our body before our mind can make sense of the emotion. So paying attention to our body can bring us closer to understanding our intuitive sense quicker. We can use our journal to explore how our intuitions come to us, and by becoming more aware of and curious about our physical responses we can short circuit the usual neural pathways, and explore new possibilities for ourselves.

Exercise 13 – Greet your body
Take a moment to feel what is going on in your body. Sit comfortably and close your eyes. Then take a tour of your body from the tips of your toes up to the top of your head.

Notice where you are holding any tension: you may choose to let it go. Make a distinction between what feels truly comfortable and what is rather habitual e.g. how you hold your stomach muscles, your brow, or the set of your jaw.

As you take a mental tour, find a way to greet each part of your body. It may be the first time you have ever thought of your body as part of who you are. You are effectively creating a new relationship with it, so be friendly!

It's strange to imagine our body as an important informational resource. If someone were to ask us what we think of something, chances are we don't immediately check how our breathing changes, how our muscles respond, or how our senses are affected. More likely we'll pay attention to the thoughts in our mind, which may be a hotchpotch of opinions we prepared earlier, things we've heard in the media, things we think the other wants to hear, or things we think we ought to think. That is, anything *but* our authentic truth.

We have become so adept at intellectualising our reactions and using our conscious rational brains to work things out, that we often overlook the fact that something smells bad, feels oppressive, or even causes our facial muscles to contract into a smile. Imagine the joy we might bring to someone if we were to tell them they make us smile. Or how much money and waste we could save by paying attention to the way something smells rather than to the printed label with the sell-by date. And maybe we need to take a rain-check on the person whose presence makes it seem difficult to breathe, or who gives us heart palpitations – and not in a good way.

The crucial new behaviour here is to make our body the first port of call. If in response to the question "how does that make me feel?" we focussed on our physical responses rather than on our intellectual analysis, we will perhaps arrive at a more truthful picture more quickly. We will certainly draw a different conclusion than we may have done by relying on our intellect alone.

Our journal is the perfect place to record new things we are noticing about our body's intelligence when we first start to pay attention to it.

How our brains deceive us

It may come as a surprise at first to notice how different our mental message is from that coming from our body. Again, this is down to the fact that our brains process things along well-worn connections, which often overlook or block an awareness of anything that is new or unexpected. In his outstanding book, The Master and his Emissary, psychiatrist Iain McGilchrist presents a compelling case for the way the left hemisphere of the brain has come to dominate in all aspects of Western culture and society. This is the part of the brain that enables us to use language, to make use of tools, to organise and categorise facts and analyse things by their constituent parts. Where the left hemisphere dominates, explains McGilchrist, we are left with a mechanical, artificial, utilitarian and fragmented view of the world. Whereas:

"The right hemisphere prioritises whatever actually is, and what concerns us. It prefers existing things, real scenes and stimuli that can be made sense of in terms of the lived world, whatever it is that has meaning and value for us as human beings."

The right hemisphere delivers a more holistic view of lived experience. It is also the region of our brain that has greater affinity for our emotional and intuitive responses, though it is possible, on McGilchrist's analysis, that this part of our cerebral function is largely over-ridden in the West.

Our mindset is very much subject to how we've been conditioned to think, overlaid by our fears and anxieties about what others might think of us, and a powerful concern about not making ourselves look weak and vulnerable. Our brain has evolved to orientate us towards choices and decisions that keep us safe, and tread the familiar path of experience. Meanwhile our spirit, intuition or physical intelligence, is telling us something different. The sense of internal struggle that results is a familiar symptom in modern life of the disconnection between our mind and our body.

We can begin to reintegrate our mental and physical intelligence by paying attention to our body's responses. Using a journal is a good analogy of the link between thought and physical action, as our imaginations wander and our hand manipulates the pen on the page. As we write our intuitive and our rational senses begin to form new connections, and become better related to each other. In this way we create a more balanced conscious environment where our brains don't deceive us quite as much.

"Holistic communion" – strengthening the mind-body link

It's one thing to check in with our body to find out how it's feeling in response to a situation in our lives. It is entirely another thing to engage our physical experience in a conversation to reveal its true message to us. This is an exercise I refer to as 'communing.'

At my journaling workshops when I introduce the idea of writing a conversation with a part of our body, a feeling or a painful symptom, there is usually a sharp intake of breath and lots of puzzled faces. It sounds weird – how can our body speak to us? How can we commune with it, have a conversation with it, and simultaneously write it as it happens?

However, if we trust the process, and allow the words to flow through our pen without censure or judgement, we can open ourselves to our deepest wisdom and insights, and receive them quite comfortably and easily. The idea is not to think too hard. In fact it's best to distract our analytical brain with something in order to let the conversation flow. Using an opening line such as "Hello (*body part or feeling or pain*) – what have you got to tell me?" provides the initial invitation that satisfies the more conventional part of our brain and permits it to drop its inhibitions! Then, once the invitation has been made it can be surprising just how readily and directly our physical, intuitive intelligence responds, and the conversation can begin.

Again, the structure-loving left-brain can be distracted by presenting the conversation rather like the script of a play, and by placing a time-limit on how long it will last. The most powerful insights are possible in a very short space of time using this journaling method, so a time-limit of 5 minutes writing is not unreasonable for a truly valuable exchange. The trick is getting out of our own way. If we do, the words that form are exactly the ones we need. They arise from the intuitive intelligence of our body and are untainted by the multiple layers of critical, analytical interpretation that our minds do so well.

In the workshops, after the puzzlement come the gasps of amazement. It really doesn't take very long to arrive at new understanding and new courses of action when we pay close attention to our body's message.

Susan came to a workshop carrying lots of tension in her neck and shoulders. Five minutes into the 'communing' exercise, once the scepticism had subsided a bit, she suddenly declared "Gosh – I've just broken through something that's been bugging me for years."

These are important moments, which give us fresh insights into new and different ways of being in our lives. They are transformative moments which show us that relying too heavily on our intellect and our thoughts doesn't always serve us. Rather it can send us round and round in circles, which often can exacerbate our physical tensions and pain. Using our journal to inquire directly of our body's message helps us to relate to our body as much more than a vehicle to carry around our head, and deepens our awareness of our physical resourcefulness.

Exercise 14 - Communing

Spend a few moments tuning in to your body. Run an inventory check from the tips of your toes to the top of your head. How does it feel? Is there any pain or tension? Is there any sensation you've been ignoring?

Bring your awareness to your physical experience.

In your journal, greet your body/tension or feeling. Perhaps ask it its name.

Then ask it what is has to tell you today. What is the message your body has for you?

Allow the words to flow. Once your body has responded, ask the next question that occurs to you. Write down the questions and answers on separate lines, and indicate which "voice" is speaking throughout the conversation.

Choosing the movies of your mind

Without a deeper awareness of our bodies, we tend to live entirely in our heads, chasing our tails with our thinking, and often being chased by our incessant mind-chatter. By changing our perspective about our thinking, and realising that "we are not our thoughts", we can loosen our attachment to our thoughts by just a touch. We can then become more physically centred, and much more objective in the choices we make. It also becomes easier not to take things too personally.

Mind or thought movies are not really about journaling – although there is nothing stopping you from writing down your thought movie if you can keep up with it. To run a thought movie is more about becoming an observer of the constant screenplay that reels in our heads. By becoming an observer, we are then able to detach ourselves from the screenplay that's running. Eventually we are able to choose to change the reel at will to view a different movie instead.

In the context of journal writing, practising thought-movies is actually about meditating to calm the mind, to create space, detachment and objectivity, and to free our writing practice from the habitual scenes that have played themselves over and over in our heads.

Imagine trying to get to sleep at night, but the mind chatter won't stop. The overactive brain keeps rabbiting on about anything and everything, or starts running horror films which ensure that we don't rest. We often refer to this experience as being a physical struggle, causing us to toss and turn in our beds. In the morning we feel groggy and exhausted, having been tortured overnight by our incessant thinking.

Of course, one way to combat this is to keep our journal by our bed, and scribble down and out of our head whatever it is that that is keeping us awake.

Alternatively you could select a thought-movie – the first few holes of golf you've played that day, the one about your wedding, the time you fell in love or the story about your last holiday in the sun. Whatever peaceful, calming movie you can choose to relax you and stop the chatter – just pop in the tape, sit back and enjoy.

The sitting back bit is important. You don't need to take part in this movie. You don't need to fight it; it's already wrapped so there's nothing you can do to change it. There's no room here for should haves or if-onlys. All you can do is allow the scenes to wash over you as you watch them play out on the giant screen of your consciousness.

Without sitting back and creating a sense of detachment, it is impossible to make choices. An enhanced sense of choice is an important by-product of our reflective writing practice. We can choose our thoughts. We can choose the things we pay attention to. We still choose by not choosing. We can choose whether or not we will be pulled by our thoughts, or whether or not we will take the opportunity to develop greater objectivity.

So, practise playing a few thought-movies from time to time. It is a way of creating space for the imagination and the intuition to roam unimpeded.

Exercise 15 – Thought-movie
Sit comfortably and close your eyes. Allow your breathing to settle into a relaxed rhythm without forcing.

Bring to mind the things you have been involved with over the past day, week or month. Picture your activities, and watch the thought movie of your life in the past period of time.

Resist the temptation to analyse or judge what you are viewing in your mind's eye. Simply allow the thoughts to pass over your internal screen.

Maybe some memories will repeat themselves. Maybe others will feel painful. Just let them go and watch for the next ones to come along. There is no need to follow them as they pass. Just sit still and observe.

Dream-logging
We are beginning to see that diving in to our inner reality through our journals helps us to discover ever deepening levels of resourcefulness. It is not just our mental capacity which dictates the extent of our imagination and creativity; we are beginning to appreciate the roles our physical intelligence and intuition play too.

A further rich resource for our personal development and understanding lies in our dreams, where creative writers might also look for story ideas. Often we will have a vivid dream whose atmosphere and imagery continue to haunt us after waking. Occasionally our dreams make us laugh out loud. More frequently perhaps they unsettle us, or reflect a circumstance or attitude in our waking lives which is troubling us.

For me personally there is nothing supernatural about dreams. I do not believe that they predict the future, nor am I superstitious about the dreams I have. Nevertheless I find dreams to be tremendously enlightening about my state of mind, and about the choices I'm facing at any given time.

Western culture tends to dismiss dreaming as an unimportant aspect of life. It happens during sleep, is clearly not "real", and therefore is not to be of any concern.

Other cultures and traditions around the world take a different view, and foster a respectful curiosity about what dreams hold.

If we take the view that our dreams are the workings of our sub-conscious mind, processing the myriad sensations, impressions and experiences our minds have formed during our life's waking hours, then it is worth in the very least getting curious about what we see when our eyes are closed and our minds are resting. Writing dreams down helps us to record them and detach ourselves from them. They need to be free-written, with absolutely no interpretation at first, ideally the moment we wake.

They are not subject to linear time, and are frequently little more than a series of tableaux, images, scenes or feelings that have come to us during sleep. As such, logging them requires even less structure than an ordinary free-written journal entry.

The moment we start worrying about spelling or punctuation or proper sentences, our critical brain is far too awake to allow the dream to be faithfully logged.

Once the dream is written down, it is available to be reflected upon. We might find obvious metaphors in the dream which reflect our current situation, or we may have to trawl deeper into our past experience to understand the substance of the dream. An important question to ask ourselves when reflecting on our dream is how it makes us feel. This gives us a journaling start-point, and begins to unlock the insights our dream might bring.

It might also be useful to initiate a conversation with a dream character, image or feeling. Our journals are great receptacles for all kinds of inquiries, and engaging our dreams in conversation to ask explicitly about the message they have for us can eliminate all kinds of speculation!

Chapter 5

Foundering

Any seasoned sea-farer will tell you that life on the open ocean is not always plain-sailing. There are times when frightening challenges are thrown up, when tragedy strikes or when the wind is quite literally taken out of our sails and we're stuck in the doldrums, unable to move.

In this chapter I will address how we can use our journals to disentangle ourselves, and use our private writing to clarify what makes us stuck, and how to get unstuck. This section also contains exercises which may be useful when life gets really bleak. Bereavement, illness, and separation are all experiences which cripple us with unimaginable grief, and it's during these times that our journal can be a valuable source of support and a means by which we can rebuild our inner resilience.

The things that hold us back
As a personal development coach I have encountered many clients who bring issues that are fundamentally similar even though the context of them and the personality harbouring them are unique in each case. Often people come to coaching to help build their self-confidence, or to help them achieve a particular goal. Always the things that are stopping them moving forward include one or all of the following:

- a confused view of themselves, their experience and potential;
- a hugely inflated sense of the task ahead;
- a virulent, poisonous line in self-sabotage.

Coaching in itself employs powerful techniques to challenge clients' action or inaction. However journal writing is also an extremely useful tool to help us raise our conscious awareness of the habitual stories, excuses, self-justifications and inaccurate perceptions that can be so crippling.

Finding the key to unlock our resistance lies in heightening our awareness of:

- what triggered it in the first place;
- what stories we've been telling and excuses we've been making ever since;
- who we are blaming;
- alternative points of view;
- what the current facts are;
- what's possible next.

Journal writer's story

Mary has a deep fear of water, stemming, she believes, from being pushed into the pool by her swimming instructor at the age of eight. As a result, for more than fifty years Mary has never been swimming, and daren't even paddle at the water's edge.

The experience she had was so traumatic it sent emotional repercussions down the years, and Mary has never been able to allow herself to enjoy swimming with her children or grandchildren. However, no matter how terrifying the event was at the time, it is not inevitable that the experience should lead to a lifetime where swimming as a healthy and enjoyable activity is a total impossibility.

Unfortunately Mary hasn't only been the victim of dubious teaching practices. She has also been the innocent victim of her own habitual story-telling. It is not the experience itself which put Mary off swimming for life, but the powerful logical narrative she created about the event, repeating it ad infinitum over the years, constantly reinforcing her resistance and fear. As an excuse not to get wet, her traumatic story has served her very well.

Now in late middle age, and suffering with arthritic joints, Mary has been asked by her doctor to consider swimming as a beneficial non-weight bearing exercise. Suddenly, the need to conquer her fear and get into the water is beginning to outweigh the fear itself, but Mary is at a loss to know where to begin.

Exercise 16 – Disentangling

The aim of this exercise is to unpick the separate strands of the real experience that may have become tangled up or lost sight of during the habitual recounting of our story. By making clear distinctions between the various elements we can deal with each one separately.

If like Mary you have a difficult experience in your past to which you attribute your current fear and resistance, give yourself permission to take up your journal and write a full-on, no holds barred technicolour account of what happened.

Don't forget to get physical – use all your senses to describe what you went through, how it felt, before, during and after.

Write down your memories of who was involved, how they reacted and what the immediate impact was on you.

As you write, notice any aspects of the experience that you may have suppressed over the years.

How does your written account differ from your habitual story about what happened?

- *In what ways has your story about the event been serving you?*
- *In what ways has it held you back?*
- *What conclusions are you beginning to draw about the true source of your resistance?*

In Mary's case, by writing a graphic account of her memory of the unfortunate swimming lesson, she became aware of the exhilaration she felt, the relief when her toes touched the bottom of the pool, and she admitted screaming with laughter when she went in. She then remembered the cruel sniggering and finger-pointing of her classmates that made her feel humiliated and small. She also realised that these are all details that she had lost sight of in all the years of relating the story about why she doesn't swim. Eventually she began to question whether it was really the water that scared her, or the possibility that she might make a fool of herself.

Only in our journal does this rediscovery and reappraisal become possible. It couldn't happen during our normal telling of the story, which has become too habitual, and which people receive with the polite sympathy and affirming understanding that only goes to reinforce even further the fictional chain of events.

Forgiving others so we can move on

Another feature of our habitual stories and "reasons why" we don't allow ourselves to experience things in life can be to do with the way we continue to hold individuals responsible for our difficulties. We might not even realise who it is that we are habitually blaming, or we might have a very clear picture of the person, and an excruciating memory of what they did to us. The fact is that harbouring blame of the person we perceive to have wronged us is a deeply insidious way of keeping our difficult experiences alive, even though they may be a long time in the past. This habit perpetuates in us the mindset of having been the victim of another's actions, damaging our sense of self-esteem and self-confidence.

In order to recover our sense of self-worth and move on without feeling like a victim any longer, a key step to take is to forgive the person we've been blaming for years.

The process of restorative justice - where perpetrators of criminal or anti-social acts get to hear directly from their victim about the impact of their actions, and where victims are able to understand some of the perpetrator's circumstances around the incident - operates on the principles of mutual understanding and forgiveness. Our journals can be a place where we conduct our own restorative justice procedure, releasing others from the blame we have been perpetually casting over them, and restoring our own sense of peace, resilience and self-belief.

Here's what Mary has to say:

"I realise that I've been bad-mouthing my old swimming instructor for years, and no doubt scores of other non-swimming adults have been doing the same. He must have been the butt of an awful lot of bad karma in his life-time! In the deep recesses of my memory I'm becoming slightly aware of once telling my best friend that I hoped Mr F. drowned. I suddenly hope that this never proved to be the case, and that he enjoyed a comfortable retirement in a cosy bungalow in view of the sea!"

Exercise 17 – RSVP

Once you have become aware of a more forgiving point of view about your nemesis you can start to put yourself in their shoes and use your journal to write their version of events, from their perspective. To get going on this, invite the person you have in mind to offer their explanation.

You might use an inquiry such as "I wonder what Mr F. thinks of this?", or a direct question "What do you have to say for yourself Mr F.?", or you might even write them an entire letter to outline your predicament, and invite the person to reply.

Here's Mr F.'s reply that Mary found herself writing:

"Dear Mary

I am utterly devastated to learn about your terrifying experience in my swimming lesson, and your on-going fear of water. It was never ever my intention to prevent you from gaining confidence in the pool – in fact quite the opposite.

The technique I used to encourage children to swim might have appeared a bit cruel, but it was a hell of a lot better to get them to use their innate ability to stay afloat rather than do what I had to do as a boy and thrash about on the poolside pretending to swim on dry land before getting a sense of being in the water. Apart from anything else it worked for the majority of children, and the smiles on their faces when they managed to tread water are what I'll never forget.

Of course my intentions were always good. I was always confident that none of my pupils were ever in danger, because I was always on hand to help them out of difficulties. I had absolute faith in everyone's ability to keep themselves afloat if they had to – not to mention the fact that we were at the shallow end of the pool and every single child *was tall enough to touch the bottom with their feet and still keep their head above the water."*

The critical piece, having written a letter such as this, is to reflect on it some more. By taking a more holistic view of a situation we are able to gain deeper insights into what might be possible next.

New possibilities

What are the current facts? In Mary's case she is clear that she cannot swim. She is adamant that this is a fact.

However, if challenged on the absolute truth of this statement she becomes less assertive. Is it absolutely true to say she cannot swim, that she has absolutely no ability to swim whatsoever?

Mary responds:

"When it's put like that I find my memory reverting back to a fleeting feeling of buoyancy, the split second ability to keep my head above the water.

Suddenly to say I cannot swim doesn't feel entirely accurate. Suddenly it feels more accurate to say I will not swim. This is the true fact of the matter. I have spent a life-time wilfully refusing to swim because of the excuses I've been making - and blaming poor Mr F.!"

So now Mary has two choices. Either she changes her will and says "For the sake of my health, I will swim. I will have a go." Or she remains convinced that

71

swimming is something she will not do, regardless of the benefits.

Exercise 18 – Absolute truths
Here's a series of questions to work through in your journal to get beyond your current stuckness and identify new possibilities.

- *What are the current facts?*
- *What is absolutely true for me right now?*
- *What are my choices?*
- *What will I do?*
- *By when will I do it?*

Another inner handbrake
As well as our habitual stories, another plague on our progress can be our inner handbrake – the critical voice that likes to tell us what we cannot and must not do in order to make ourselves truly happy.

The inner critic is our brain's way of keeping us safe. It is our inbuilt resistance to any type of change which might put us in jeopardy. The trouble is our inner critic frequently masquerades as our voice of reason and in this way manages to make itself utterly convincing.

Typical things that I hear my inner critic say are: "You can't do that; I'd like to see the outcome of that little venture; ten bad marks!; who do you think you are?; that's a bit weird; that's a bit over the top; but how will you make any money?"

We all have the experience of talking ourselves out of something that seemed like a good idea at the time. We have an inner mechanism which prefers sitting on the sofa to going for a run; or opening a monthly pay cheque to following our dreams (as if the two things need to be mutually exclusive.)

The journal is the perfect place to expose our inner critic once and for all. By shining our mental spotlight on the arguments we often use to dissuade ourselves from doing something different with our lives, we can begin to unpick the crippling work of our inner critical voice.

Exercise 19 – Get to know your inner critic

Spend a few moments listening for your own inner critic's voice. You may find it to be a very familiar sound. (Be careful - you may even think that it's actually your own voice. Be wary of the inner critic that's inveigled its way into your repertoire to such a degree that you've lost sight of where you end and it begins.)

Make a note in your journal of the typical things you hear in your head that stop you from doing what you want to do, or expressing the ideas you'd like to express. Who is speaking these things?

- *Write a pen portrait of the character to whom these phrases belong.*
- *What would you like to do with this inner critic?*
- *(I like to imagine shoving an old sock into its mouth and tying it to a chair!)*
- *What are you grateful for in this character?*
- *(I'm grateful for its sardonic doubt which gives me the kick up the backside I need to move me forward sometimes!)*

Exercise 20 – Job description

Interestingly, the last thing we want to do with our inner critic is to engage it in too much conversation. We don't want to give it too much of a voice. Rather we want to put a stop to its robbing us of our voice.

So stay in control and write your inner critic a job description. Outline its duties very clearly, and point out when its views will be welcomed and when they will not.

If we can get to see the benign side of our inner critic we usually find that it just wants the best for us after all, and actually wants to protect us. We can take active steps to quieten down the inner critic by making sure we ourselves are going about the changes we want to see in our life in a safe and responsible way.

The curveballs of life
Bereavement, grief, illness, family breakdown, divorce and redundancy are all events in our lives which knock us off track. At these times our journals provide a place for us to express ourselves and our pain, to rant, get angry, swear, or just write down all that we miss and are grateful for.

Writing a letter to a loved one who has passed away, and then receiving their reply, ensures that we carry their voice and their wisdom with us on our continuing journey through life. It can be extremely cathartic.

Writing creatively about an item that belonged to our loved one, that they particularly cherished or enjoyed can give us an access point into their life and experience that can deepen our appreciation of them.

When things feel too painful to write in the first person, or when our grief is so deep it feels like we have no life left at all to call our own, we can begin to think of new possibilities by referring to ourselves as he or she. Writing in the third person helps us go easy on ourselves. It helps us maintain perspective by creating a little bit of space and detachment between ourselves and our experience. It also helps us to move on. Our loss will never be replaced, but eventually we can leave behind the sadness and gradually consider new possibilities. Sometimes it's easier to pretend that the possibilities will be for someone else.

Summary
Our journals free us up from the habitual stories and blame of our past and enable us to restore our own sense of self-worth to meet new challenges and opportunities. Reflective writing also affords us the objectivity and perspective to identify the critical voice that continues to hold us back in the present. And when tragedy strikes our journals are havens for us to deepen our inner reserves and develop a greater appreciation and gratitude for those we have lost.

Chapter 6

Discovering the Buried Treasure

In the childhood voyages of our dreams there would always be buried treasure to be discovered on our travels. There would be a map, usually of a desert island, and x would mark the spot where we would start digging.

To find the treasure is the purpose of our voyage. And we do not find it unless we dig. In journaling terms our buried treasure is our authentic wisdom and insightfulness which guides us to do things our own way, and which shows us the right place to dig. If we manage to get out of our own way what we find always surprises us.

Billy says:

"During a low point in my life, I used journal writing as a release, and a way of getting my multitude of thoughts and emotions down. Mostly it didn't have the immediate impact that I was craving, but it did sow seeds for further clarity, calmness and understanding that was essential to me moving on from the dark place.

The insight came months later when I was reading back over what I had written. Often I was more insightful than I remembered being at the time, or conversely completely lagging behind where I thought I was."

Reading back through the journaling entries he wrote in the dark place, Billy is surprised by the accuracy of the insights he finds, and at times by the falseness of his writing. Without reflecting on what he had written previously he would neither have discovered the buried treasure in his writing – nor the decoys that he had planted, fully believing at the time that these were also authentic nuggets.

He is beginning to be aware of the different voices that emerge at times in our journal, depending perhaps on the degree of emotion that we are experiencing, and on the degree to which we are trying desperately to protect ourselves from our own vulnerabilities.

It is difficult to describe the nature and the effect of each of our voices when we reflect on what we've written. Perhaps the easiest way is to notice how reflecting on our writing makes us feel. In my experience my most authentic journal entries feel right to me; they have a quiet logic, a balanced perspective, and an awareness and acceptance of my vulnerability. They show self-respect, and make perfect sense.

Exercise 21 – Hidden voices
Read back through earlier entries in your journal. Reflect on the following questions as you read:

- *What does the writing indicate about your state of mind at the time?*
- *How does re-reading the entry make you feel?*
- *What appears to be the dominant voice in earlier entries – your ego, your inner critic, your wisdom, or something else?*
- *What are the distinguishing features of each voice?*
- *In what ways do earlier entries move you forward?*
- *In what ways do they perpetuate the illusion of moving forward?*

Authenticity and Integrity
It is a curious phenomenon that developing a regular journal writing practice will automatically encourage us to express ourselves in a thoroughly genuine way.

When we are writing for ourselves it becomes impossible to keep up any of the personae or mini-dramas we indulge in with others around. As one of my workshop participants put it so pithily "there's nowhere to hide when you are writing to yourself."

There is no need to try and keep up appearances in our journal. It is a place like no other in which we can explore and reflect on what is truly happening under the surface of our lives, where we can catch ourselves "in the act" and get curious about it.

Exercise 22 – Ranting #1
Whenever there is something that is making you really angry and frustrated allow yourself to take up your journal and write down your thoughts and feelings. Don't hold back. Allow yourself to rant about the situation, what someone else has done, how far they are to blame, how they've made you feel.

Repeat this exercise for a few minutes every day for 7 days. Write with abandon.

Notice the point at which you begin to feel that your anger and frustration are no longer real, when it feels hard work to rant, and it feels like you are making it up, forcing it.

Reading back over what you have written what weakness is your writing trying to cover up?

Also notice what other voice is beginning to reveal itself. What insights is it showing you?

Ranting #2
I recently learned this approach to ranting from psychologist Sarah Rozenthuler, who states that RANT is an acronym for Resent, Appreciate, Need, Truth. By allowing ourselves to write down what we resent about someone, then what we appreciate about them, and then what we need from them, we will become more focused on the truth of our feelings. This is a useful way of staying in integrity with ourselves and avoiding

emotional outbursts during which we might say things we will later regret.

The strength in vulnerability

It is frequently the case that we discover our authentic voice when we are prepared to accept and explore our own vulnerability and weaknesses. Not that weakness needs to be perceived in any pejorative sense. Having weaknesses doesn't make us "less than", it doesn't need judgment, it just needs acceptance and recognition. It also needs ownership. As long as we own our vulnerability and weaknesses, and take responsibility for them, we will not only make ourselves stronger, we will also be encouraged to discover an alternative approach that rings truer for us.

Journal writer's story

Peter runs a small oven-cleaning business. He is fantastic at delivering the service his customers need, but is not quite so effective in marketing his services or making the sale. He very clearly thinks of this as his weakness.

He writes:

"There's so much pressure out there to ramp up marketing and sales. So many gurus telling me I need to be doing more networking, cold-calling and canvassing. Of course I feel the pressure to make more sales myself as well – I need to make a living from this job! So I'm running a bit scared at the moment, knowing what I should be doing, but really wishing I didn't have to."

Peter is beginning to admit that he is feeling scared. In his writing he is allowing his honest feelings to come through and to recognise where he feels vulnerable.

He writes:

"I guess I've got my head in the sand. Ha! Never really saw myself as an ostrich!! There must be a better way. Come to think of it I quite like what John does with his marketing. He makes it look so easy and natural. Maybe that's what I need to find. Something that feels easy and natural for me..."

Immediately he has admitted that he's been avoiding the problem, and opened himself up to what else might be possible, his writing reveals that an idea has come to him straight away in the guise of his friend John who also runs his own small business.

He is starting to get curious about what's going to work for him, so instead of feeling overwhelmed and terrified by everything the marketing gurus will tell him to do, he's going to be able to make more discerning choices. He's going to be able to take a more dispassionate view of John's approach, to see what he might learn from him, instead of running scared from his competitors.

Taking this line of ownership, being responsible for his perceived weakness in marketing and sales, and allowing himself to get curious about his vulnerability instead of sticking his head in the sand, Peter is able to identify a more authentic line of action for himself. Here's his journal entry from just a couple of days later:

"Been having a good think about this sales and marketing malarkey. Took another look at what it is John does and had a look through a few marketing blogs online. Not all of it sat well with me but there are at least three things I've picked up that I can be doing better. I need to be more proactive with my existing customers. I usually wait for them to call me but I guess I could make things easier for them if I gave them a call to see if they want to book another appointment. Life gets hectic for everyone and sometimes it's good to get a prompt. Another thing is I'm going to try leafleting in a few streets. Terry can do me a good deal on printing so I could drop some leaflets then follow up with a quick door to door to see if anyone would like more information. I don't mind chatting to people and that's all this is really. So there's my plan: phone existing customers, drop some leaflets and follow up. Can't believe it's taken me so long to work this out.. Can't wait to get started now."

Following this Peter made an extra six sales in three weeks, and four of them came from making the extremely simple first step of contacting existing customers. His intuition was correct, they'd all been meaning to get back to him but had been so busy they hadn't had chance. They were all delighted to hear from him and really grateful for the call.

What's more, by playing to his strength of chatting to people Peter really began to raise his profile in the local area. Of course he got a few doors slammed in his face, but he didn't get put off. He understood that chatting to people is not for everyone!

One lady told him that a couple of friends of hers were recently asking if she knew of any oven cleaners so Peter was able to pass on his details. The following week someone from the other side of town phoned to book an appointment.

In a very short time, using readily available resources at minimum cost, and a few moments' reflection in his journal, Peter discovered an authentic solution to his problem and a more discerning and natural approach to his sales and marketing issues.

Exercise 23 – Taking ownership
Consider the following inquiries in your journal:

- *Where am I most vulnerable?*
- *What am I avoiding?*
- *What's my intention?*
- *What support do I need?*
- *What action can I take immediately to move forward?*

Words of warning

In Billy's example earlier he noticed how some of his writing during his lowest point somehow lagged behind where he thought he was at the time. As he reflects he detects that there is something not quite right or real about his words.

Sometimes we might discover that our treasure map contains a decoy, a false trail that has been laid by that most fearful part of ourselves, our ego or inner critic. Typically such a trail leads us into a trap – either one which protects us from admitting our own vulnerability and discovering some truth; or one which perpetuates the illusion that writing is doing.

In my journal I cringe at the sections which have a strange pleading energy, or a desperate sense of trying to be convincing. These are the passages where the style is somehow trying too hard, with too many words, ideas that aren't really my own, and too much skirting around an issue.

When I read and reflect on these sections of my journal I become impatient, agitated and slightly ashamed. And if I'm not careful my inner critic starts screaming something like "you haven't got time for this journal nonsense – stop navel gazing and start doing..."

Writing in our journal is no substitute for doing real things in our lives. Reflective writing might help us determine which pots need to be washed, but it isn't going to wash them for us. Our journals can help us get clarity on what our next actions need to be, but we still have to perform the actions ourselves in order to move forward and make a difference.

Imagine sitting at a dressing table with two hinged mirrors. With the mirrors at an open angle before you it is possible to see two separate reflections of yourself. However as you move the mirrors closer together, the number of reflections increases in proportion to the decreasing angle of the hinges, until it is possible to see an infinite number of reflections tunnelling away from you in either direction.

This optical experiment is a useful metaphor for what happens when we become too introspective. The reflections before us are increasingly illusory and bring their own brand of tunnel vision to our thought process.

In the same way that the light rebounds within the system of mirrors, we are at risk of recreating in our journals the experience of going round in circles, beating ourselves up about the things we're not achieving, and writing ever more furiously and ineffectually.

Getting real

Reflective journal writing is not an excuse for locking ourselves away in the ivory tower of our inaction. Whenever this happens we need to shift ourselves. We need to do something different to break out of our intellectual delusion and reconnect ourselves with the real world of physical effects and outcomes.

We may choose to get up and move about, get some exercise, prune the roses, do some ironing or practice some yoga. Our bodies can help us shake ourselves out of our heads, and out of the endless cycles of mental chatter.

Better still we might put down our pen and do the thing we've been most putting off, that's nevertheless been blocking our progress to what we want to achieve. We can consciously and whole-heartedly choose to tidy our office or make that phone call or knuckle down to our latest project.

Keeping a journal is not always about escaping. Rather it is about heightening our personal integrity and identifying where we can take the most straightforward and meaningful actions in the real world.

Journal writer's story

Hill-walker Marie was recovering from a serious illness, and lacking confidence about her ability to keep up with her fellow hikers. However she was determined to coach herself into action, and used her journal to prepare for her next climb:

I was sitting in my kitchen looking out at the hills and thinking about the next Munro that I would be climbing that weekend. I decided that the majority of my perceived weakness was all in my mind and that if I could change my way of thinking that I could have a more positive experience and overcome my shortcomings.

I started writing and really just let the words flow across the page. At first, the words would not come however the more I let my mind rest, the more relaxed I became. I started by writing statements regarding how far I had come. What I had achieved etc. From this I began to visualise myself climbing the hill at a pace that was enjoyable to me. What was I seeing, how did I feel. This was translated into words within my journal. Before long I had completed a couple of pages of writing and I was feeling extremely positive about the whole experience. I could keep up, I was good enough. I was there to enjoy myself. I had only just started and my energy levels and focus were improving with each outing. Instead of concentrating on others, I was truly focused on me and what I was achieving. The whole experience was very moving and filled me with a warmth that I will never forget.

When I looked back at what I had written, I was amazed. I believe the words were written from my heart. I did not consciously write good feeling thoughts. When I allowed the response to flow, and did not force the act, something inside me just took over. I believe I honestly spoke to myself from deep inside.

Exercise 24 – The golden thread of integrity
Read back through earlier entries in your journal.

- What are the particular values and strengths that you identify from your writing?
- What is the thread of integrity that runs through the entries that is always true for you?
- Spend five minutes responding to the kick-off phrase: "The treasure I have found within myself is…"

Chapter 7

Safe moorings

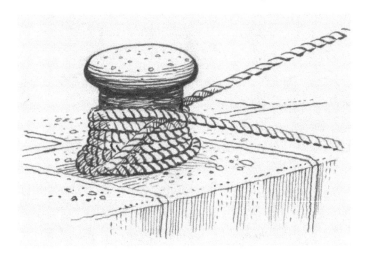

Whatever voyage we're on we always have to find a safe harbour in which we can replenish our stocks and refresh our crew. It is a vital aspect of our journey that we give ourselves time to relax, reflect and recover from our experiences so far. It's also a time when we need to take on fresh food and water, resources that will sustain us as we continue on our journey.

Finding safe mooring to review our progress in our journal is an extremely illuminating and valuable part of our reflective writing practice.

Reviewing progress

Reflecting back on all we have achieved and experienced over a preceding period of time is a great way to understand what direction we're heading in, and to refocus on what's important for the coming "voyage". It also enables us to let go of what's passed with gratitude and express our hopes and intentions for the next period of time.

Irene says:

"Writing once a month helps me focus on what I have achieved rather than what I still want to do or don't have. I never realised how much I did achieve until I started sitting down at the end of the month, getting out the diary and writing in my journal. It has been an amazing process for me."

It may seem paradoxical, but looking backwards can help us move forwards. Reflecting and reviewing enable us to look back and within to understand more thoroughly what is possible next. It's a different process from goal setting and project planning, which tend to be activities that focus on external factors and on what there is still to do. When we focus on what we still don't have or still haven't achieved, it robs us of the opportunity to celebrate and be grateful for all that we have done. It causes us to miss so much of our own experience and potential, and holds us in a place of lack rather than of abundance.

According to the Law of Attraction, the more we tell ourselves that we want something, the more we are emphasising our current lack of that thing. It's far better to emphasise what we are grateful for, and focus our intention on creating a present reality that will attract those things into our life that are not currently there. The only way to do this is to be completely present, to savour every moment of our experience and bring our best to it. We know what our best is by familiarising ourselves with our authentic voice through journal writing, and we can set our intentions from a place of integrity and confidence once we truly begin to appreciate all that we have already achieved.

Exercise 25 – Snapshots

Journaling snapshots are reflective writing sessions that occur at the close of a specific period of time. Decide what your own optimal time-split is – is it daily, weekly, monthly or quarterly – when you can realistically spare 20 minutes to sit down, reflect on your achievements over the period and write about them in your journal.

Learn to look forwards to and relish your regular snap-shot time with your journal. You may even decide to invest in a new notebook to serve the purpose.

I have a snapshot journal in which I reflect on the last day of every month, using no more than two sides of A5 for each time period, so I calculate that the notebook will last me a number of years, and contain a fascinating record of achievements, expressions of gratitude and lessons learned.

Once you have your notebook and have determined your own particular "time-split" you may find the following inquiries and kick-off phrases help:

- *"My biggest lesson was..."*

- *"The main event for me has been.."*
- *"I am most grateful for..."*
- *"What have I achieved?"*
- *"What have I learned?"*
- *"The intention I am forming is..."*

You may also consider writing your snap-shot as a list - your 50 distinct achievements or lessons or insights or delights.

Snap-shots remind us about the cyclical nature of our experience, and connect us to a particular rhythm and routine that helps to stabilise and centre ourselves. This equates to the constant need to find safe mooring to rest and replenish ourselves ready for the next leg of our journey.

Resistance is futile!

At times, it is a struggle to persuade ourselves to drop anchor for a bit and take some time to reflect on our experience so far. We feel the urge to keep battling on, resisting the need for time-out, even though we are getting exhausted, and are in grave danger of running on empty and finally stalling completely.

For me this can happen when I feel as if I haven't done enough on a particular project, if I'm dissatisfied with my output to date, or when I haven't yet arrived at the point I was hoping to achieve.

Radical action may be required to help us break out of this mindset of constant effort, especially when we're sending ourselves round in circles and are at risk of getting terminally stuck.

Although we are loath to admit it, relying on our own inner resources at this point is dangerous, as they are likely to be extremely depleted. We would not allow our crew to bypass a harbour and continue sailing if we knew that our rations were running out.

We would need to stop for a while, just long enough to refresh our hold with what we require for the next part of our trip.

Similarly with personal development and journal writing this is a time when we might look for external assistance and resources to facilitate our progress and help us reframe our situation. Quotations, images, pieces of music, or passages from our favourite book can all serve as reframing tools, something that will bring us a fresh perspective or a deeper understanding of our current situation.

One of my favourite reframing tools is the set of Medicine Cards by Jamie Sams and David Carson, which features the images and wisdom of 53 animals that are familiar to Native American culture. Tarot, angel and grace cards are also available, or look out for journal writing prompt cards, containing a kick-off phrase or inquiry to help you gain a fresh view.

There need be nothing supernatural about the way we interact with such images and tools. For me they are simply a way of engaging a different level of metaphorical thought which enables me to make new connections, find new similarities and see things more distinctly. The Medicine Cards help me personally to create the right kind of meditative and reflective environment I require to engage my intuitive mind and get well and truly under the skin of an issue that's blocking my progress.

Here's what came out in my journal at a crisis point in my book-writing progress:

26 April 2011

I need some serious help on my book project. It's been dragging on too long. I need to know what's holding me back, what's getting in my way? What is stopping me feeling the urgency of this project? What is the breakthrough I need? How am I going to discipline myself in the way that's required? What is the way that's required? What space do I need? What is going to be my first step in kick-starting this project? How am I going to stop asking, and start answering my own questions? At what point will contemplation no longer be enough – and concerted action needs to kick in?

In this case the inquiries came thick and fast as I free-wrote and became wholly focused on the frustration of feeling so blocked. These are the types of questions I held in my mind as I shuffled the Medicine Cards and resolved to draw a "Moon Lodge" spread to get centred and break any self-deceptions.

The next step after shuffling is to spread the cards face down in front of you, and intuitively choose a card or series of cards which you are inviting to help you work through your issue. The process of choosing the cards is fascinating. Once we engage our intuitive sense we find it seems impossible for our fingers to pass over the card that is right for us in the moment. In the same way that as journal writers we learn to trust that the words that come from our pen are those that are most needed, we learn to trust our intuition in guiding us to the cards that can be of most assistance to us.

As you turn over the cards the animals that are represented offer their wisdom to help you reframe and mine deeper into what's going on for you, and what's needed to break through the obstacles.

In the case of my Moon Lodge Spread, here's what happened:

27 April 2011

A very insightful spread. Reassuring me I know my own answers.

Rabbit tells me to re-evaluate in order not to be frozen in the headlights, and Bear reminds me that my answers lie within.

Prairie Dog warns me about unproductive scurrying, and challenges me to take a break and refill my resources.

Dragonfly reminds me to break down the illusions I'm harbouring that are restricting me.

Crow calls me to stop lying to myself and Spider urges me to create, to keep putting one word in front of the other and trust in the infinite possibilities there are, the endless webs I can weave.

Squirrel reminds me about abundance and tells me to stop being so erratic and to focus.

Opossum tells me to be clever and use my sense of drama and surprise.

Ant calls me to be patient and not fall foul of those who are out for their own gain.

Skunk reminds me that what I believe about myself is my ultimate protection and I need to walk my talk.

No more scurrying – time to slink!

This exercise was a great boost to me, and also prevented me from becoming unbalanced once again. Four days later I commissioned artist David Thelwell to create the illustrations for my book, and suddenly the wind caught my sails once more.

Exercise 26 – Reframing
If using a metaphorical divining system such as the Medicine Cards feels uncomfortable, you can create your own set of reframing resources. These are simply a set of metaphors that have meaning for you, and which you can draw on and ponder their wise message to you.

You can use:

- *Your favourite children's fictional character*
- *Your favourite recipe, song or image*
- *Your pets*
- *Your dreams*
- *The person who most irritates you*
- *The person who most inspires you*
- *Words you like*
- *Quotations*
- *Objects you love*

- *Objects or features from your dreams*

You may choose to create a lucky dip, and ponder your question as you stir or shake the box or hat that contains the cards or slips of paper representing your personal metaphors. You can then create a game for yourself where you draw two or three cards and see how they relate to your issue, and what they can tell you.

Alternatively, there are other reframing techniques which encourage us to think of different perspective on a particular issue. Here's what a couple of my workshop attendees had to say:

Sue uses The 5 Why's:

"It's a technique (cannot remember whose) that helps me unpick why I felt bad about a situation, and why I reacted negatively or over-emotionally. The 5 Whys help me to find what the blockages really are – and then to have insights about solutions. "

Gail says:

"For me, I think the most insightful experiences I've had through journal writing came with doing "CBT" exercises – which I first began doing using a workbook I'd bought in Waterstones. I'd bought it during a difficult period in my life, but actually found it fun, interesting and enlightening

to take a situation that I'd had an initial negative response to, or a negative emotional reaction, and write down 10 other ways I could choose to feel or choose to perceive the situation. It always makes me feel happier and also, for lack of a better word, powerful. By powerful, I mean within myself – the power to be in charge of how I feel and react, not powerful over others.

"I've done a similar thing also when making lists of blessings, when I'm feeling grumpy and put-upon. It works! Sounds soppy, but I usually find it quite humbling and energizing, too."

Getting ready for the off once again
Having taken some time out to restore our energy levels, and take stock of where we've been, we can then challenge ourselves about the next leg of our journey.

Bearing in mind our progress to date, our innermost intentions, and our current issues and what's needed to resolve them, we can reenergise ourselves with a short, punchy inquiry.

Exercise 27 – Challenge
Here are a few inquiries to use when you are safely moored and have created the space for deeper reflection. Notice none of these questions is longer than 6 words. The shorter the more powerful:

- *"What's true for me?"*

- *"What's the lie?"*
- *"What's missing?"*
- *"What must I let go of?"*
- *"Where am I selling out?"*
- *"What's a new way?"*

It is useful to allow ourselves to mull over a powerful inquiry without writing anything initially. You might choose to hold your inquiry for a few days, allowing it to percolate for you while you're doing other mundane tasks such as ironing or mowing the lawn. During this time of inquiry, pay attention to the images you see, the music you hear or what you happen to read. You may choose to use these resources as external reframing tools.

When you come to your journal, it may be helpful to respond to a kick-off phrase that refers to your inquiry.

For example:

- *"My truth is..."*
- *"The lie I keep telling myself is..."*
- *"What I need to include is..."*
- *"I'm letting go of..."*
- *"Selling out feels like..."*
- *"A new way for me is to..."*

Everything is cyclical. Once our stocks are replenished we can untie the mooring rope and be off on our next adventure, consciously buoyed along by our journals and our reflective writing practice.

Ship ahoy!

Mood Index

"We understand so little about our moods – no wonder we're moody!"

The following list of moods and meditations may help you to pinpoint how you are feeling, and provides a suggested journaling exercise to support you in getting curious about your mood or working through it to a resolution that is comfortable for you.

You will find both positive and negative moods included in this list. This is because journaling is not just about writing when you're feeling lousy. Journaling is invaluable when we're feeling on top of the world as well, as it helps us to understand the things that buoy us up and make us feel good, which then become more accessible for us when our mood swings the other way. It may even reduce the frequency of our mood swings, and shorten the length of our low mood.

You can dip into the mood index at any time, selecting the mood that most corresponds to your current state of mind, and work through the exercise.

Alternatively, you might choose the opposite mood to the one you're in and write about that. For example: If you're feeling bored and uninspired you might choose to write in answer to the inquiry "What does inspiration mean to me?" Then you explore what an inspired mood would look like to you.

If you choose a negative mood to reflect on when you're feeling positive, beware. You might want to get curious about why you want to bring yourself down, or you might want to explore your mischievous side!

This is by no means an exhaustive list of moods. Neither is it meant to be read straight through, but rather accessed as and when the mood takes you! As you get used to journaling, and to identifying your mood, you will most likely come up with your own list and corresponding exercises. Hopefully the ideas here will get you going, and help you become more familiar with your own climate of moods.

How are you feeling?

1. Active

Perhaps quite rightly the last thing you'll want to do if you're feeling active is to sit down and write in your journal. We need to make the most of our active mood to get things done, to get some exercise or make progress on an important project.

However if you want to capture this active mood in the moment, grab your journal and write quickly and in big letters the first action word that comes into your head. Set yourself a challenge, a distance or timescale.

E.g. RUN. 1 mile. NOW!

And just do it! Afterwards, take some time to reflect on your activity. What triggered it? How did it feel? Where in your body did it have most impact? How did it help? What did you achieve?

2. Afraid

Use the following kick-off phrases to name your fear.

"I'm afraid of…"

Or

"My greatest fear is…"

Write directly, allowing your pen to lead you straight to the truth. Once you have the words in front of you on the page you will have objectified your fear and let it go to some degree. It is now available for you to explore from a more helpful perspective.

At this point inquire where this fear comes from? What inner critic is taunting you? What are you called to do next?

3. Alert

An alert person is awake and aware, perhaps having heard an alarm go off, or having received a more metaphorical wake-up call.

Being alert is a great thing. It helps us forge ahead with our projects and feel fulfilled at the end of each day. It's easier to focus on important tasks, write lists and get into action.

However, unless our attention is gainfully employed and we can find a useful focus for our alert state of mind, we may have a tendency to think too much, over analyse or get ahead of ourselves and develop unrealistic goals.

So being alert is very much about being present, dealing effectively with any alarm bells that may be going off, and focussing on what we can reasonably and safely achieve right now.

Helpful inquiries might be:

- "What am I waking up to?"
- "What alarm bell is ringing?"

Always find a way to anchor this alert mood by getting curious about it. How does it feel in your body to be alert? What is your attention most immediately drawn to? What tendencies do you have to get ahead of yourself?

4. Angry

When the red mist falls there is nothing else for it – RANT! Reach for your journal and just write as fast and hard as you need to.

This is the ultimate free-writing. Allow yourself to cover pages if necessary. And if you're still angry the next day, and the next day, do the same.

But beware - don't make it into a comfortable new habit. Ring the changes by writing an angry letter to the object of your fury, or conduct an inner conversation with the offending person or thing.

At some point you will feel the anger subside. You will suddenly be aware of a new perspective becoming clear for you. You will begin to hear your voice of reason return. And it will be such a relief.

5. Anxious

Anxiety is a very distracting emotion that affects us mentally and physically. It arises when we feel insecure, and when the quality of our thinking deteriorates.

Sometimes our anxieties increase when we get tired, lose focus or find ourselves colluding with the limiting beliefs of our inner critic. Sometimes they are based on a set of circumstances that are very real to us – lack of money, concern about a family member, ill health or grief.

An inquiry to begin quelling the tide of anxiety and to start regaining some focus and control over any negative thinking would be "What is true?"

You might also try a list of blessings, or a kick-off, such as "In my life I'm most grateful for..."

6. Ashamed

Ever have any regrets about something you've said or done? Or ever had an impact on a person or a situation that's left you feeling uncomfortable?

I remember as a child the real heart-thumping feeling of guilt or shame about something I'd said or done. These days this strange, creeping feeling of shame can return when I'm doing something new or different for the first time, and I'm unsure what others might think of me. It's like the recoil after firing a shot and not being sure what damage has been done.

To be ashamed is to be remorseful, regretful, and unable to accept yourself. Taken to extremes it can result in self-hating, resisting, struggling, wanting to hide, lashing out at others, blaming and self-harming.

We can be ashamed of our actions, or something we've said or the way we have behaved. We can also feel ashamed even when we don't know what impact we've had, just because we're worried about what other people think of us and what we've done. A shameful feeling can be visceral, physical, making us want to cover our face, shake our head, hide ourselves and push others away. Shame makes us blush or itch, but it's something deeper than embarrassment, it's more about how we react when we feel judged, or when we imagine that others are judging us, or when we judge ourselves too harshly. The physical itch of shame is reflected in the medieval penance of wearing a hair shirt.

Exercises to deal with this feeling include:

- Inquiries, such as: what is my intention? What do I need to let go of? How am I judging myself? How am I imagining others are judging me?

- You might also try writing a letter to your higher self, or to a trusted person in your life, someone whom you know does not want you to feel ashamed about anything. Then, crucially, write their reply. What message do they have for you about the source of your shame?

7. Attentive

It could be argued that the best time to write in our journal is when we're in an attentive mood, when we are most likely to be paying attention to all that is around us.

However, most often if this is the case we're the last on the list, as there are too many others in our life who require our attention when it is ours to give. Children, relations, friends, colleagues, neighbours, even pets, take priority in a world where we're taught, especially if we're female, not to be selfish, and to think of others before ourselves.

We might also attend to our work, our garden, creative projects or our sports or social life, without ever reflecting on what these things give us, how we can make more time for them, or prevent them from dominating our life.

The trick is to notice what is calling for our attention in the moment and if possible to name it. Only then are we able to choose what we give our attention to. Our journal is the ideal place to jot this down and become even more consciously aware of how we spend or waste our attention.

Try noting down your response to the kick-off phrase "I am being called to..." to gauge where your attention is being pulled. Go with the flow of your attentive mood. Become more tuned in to when your attentiveness is no longer required by others. This will then free up time for you to attend to yourself and your own reflections.

8. Bored

It is extremely hard to imagine how a seasoned journal writer becomes bored in their life. This is because once we have allowed our creativity to flow in our writing we never cease running out of ideas and inspiration about things we want to do. In fact the risk, that I know only too well, is that we go to the other extreme and have so much going on that we rarely have time to pause.

Nevertheless I do recall a time when I knew so little about myself that it was very difficult to say what bored me or excited me. I tended to react to what I felt ought to be boring or exciting, according to popular preconceptions, rather than discovering real experience for myself.

The key point here is that in this modern world where we have so much leisure time on our hands, if we're bored it's probably because we haven't yet found out enough about ourselves. We really don't know what it is that makes us tick, or how capable we are. So developing a journal writing practice is the first step in finding these things out, and eliminating boredom forever!

And it is useful to write a bored list – a list of 100 things you could be doing instead of being bored.

Glancing through my list I notice things like "Take down the lounge curtains and re-gather them" which is guaranteed to make sure I never have a spare bored moment!

Alternatively my bored list has thrown up other things which I'm just not getting round to doing, but which would be great fun, and which could form the kernel of a new project, such as learning a language or how to play a challenging classical piece on the piano.

And the other benefit is that it's identified mundane things which I could get someone else to do for me, such as fixing the shower tray, which would be a weight off my mind, make me feel better, and allow another spark of inspiration to ignite.

9. Celebratory

So many people I speak to about journal writing tend to miss the opportunity to reflect on their celebratory mood because, quite rightly, they're too busy celebrating. In a similar way to how we might use our journal when we're in an active mood, logging how we feel when we're celebrating allows us to capture something delicious about our experience in the moment which will inspire us, and remind us of the joy we felt, for a long time to come.

While we're busy taking photos of the celebration we can't take a picture of our mood, our thought pattern or our state of mind. The only way to capture that and to be able to take a look at it later on is to write it down.

The journal entry can be the briefest WOOHOO, or the quickest explanation of what's happened: "Beat my personal best AGAIN!" It's also useful to note whether you're then quick to add a "but", and get curious about that, or whether you're happy to be fully in the moment of celebration.

10. Compassionate (Loving)

Compassion is such a fascinating emotion because it is multi-faceted. It can be a spontaneous response to something, and it can also be a more cultivated approach to life.

In fact the great journal pioneer of the 1970s Ira Progoff described reflective writing practice as being the art of "cultivated spontaneity", where paying regular attention to our emotional responses can lead us to satisfying and meaningful experiences. As we develop our reflective writing practice we might also recognise the importance of compassion and actively practice evoking and nurturing our compassionate responses.

The semantic root of compassion means "suffering with" and recent neuroscience demonstrates that this is a particular characteristic of intelligences whose brains feature mirror neurons that allow the individual to identify with and feel the pain of another.

The compassionate tradition has suffered a demise in our post-industrial age of consumerism, and this has led to the exploitation of our fellow human beings and the natural resources of our planet to a level which is now beyond critical. A more cultivated form of compassion is perhaps the emotion that the world needs most right now, and our journals are a perfect place for us to focus on our own compassionate responses.

- When someone really gets up your nose and you feel you could never forgive them for something, meditate on what it is you are grateful to that person for.

- In contemplating the evil deeds of an individual, ask yourself what the world looks like through their eyes. What experience have they had in their life that has brought them to this point? Then inquire "How would I feel if...?"

- Another powerful exercise is to strike up a conversation with your compassionate self, or write it a letter, and await its response. What can it help you to learn?

And remember there are some people who are so unlikeable you just have to love them instead!

11. Conflicted (Torn) (Confused) (Indecisive)

Weighing up the pros and cons of something, asking do I or don't I, and being able to see both sides of the situation, can result in very conflicted feelings. In this case, take a moment to tune into your body and familiarise yourself with how a conflicted feeling manifests itself physically. People often talk about feeling a split between their heart and their head, or feeling torn in two inside. We often talk about having our heart-strings pulled, while our head is desperately trying to pull back.

Once you've begun to recognise the physical sense of feeling conflicted, you can then begin to inquire about how you might proceed. Again the body is a useful informational resource here. We often refer to our gut feeling, our instinct, which sends us messages about how it would feel to take one course of action over another. Sometimes it's tempting to confuse our gut feeling with our fears, which are generated in our anxious brains rather than in our core.

Tuning in to our intuitive authentic voice happens naturally once we develop a regular journal writing practice. We don't need to be taught how to do this, all we need to do is allow ourselves the time and space to write and we eventually come to recognise our unique inner thread of integrity which keeps us on the right path.

Another important distinction to make is between what we are being drawn towards and what obligation is pushing us towards. If you regularly find yourself using words like should and ought, it's time to pay more attention to what is repeatedly, and sometimes annoyingly, pulling you in the opposite direction.

Try this series of inquiries:

- What is it like to be torn? How does it feel in my body?
- What does my gut say? With my feet firmly planted on the ground, what does my gut say?
- What does my authentic voice tell me?
- What does it tell me really?

Imagining and writing about the different scenarios that would result from taking one course of action over another is also a useful technique to break through indecision. Writing as the 'you' that takes the first option, what does your life look life in 3 months, 6 months, one year from now. Then, do a similar exercise writing as the 'you' that takes an alternative option.

Notice if you're tempted to write about yourself in the third person at all – this could indicate that you don't identify with the "you" that is taking one course of action over another, and might show you the option that feels most natural for you.

You might also choose to write entirely in the third person, and see what insights you glean.

12. Determined

Determination, like compassion, is one of those emotions that is worth cultivating, but which it is difficult to do until we reach a certain level of self-knowledge and self-awareness. How does my determination show up? What does it feel like? What happens when my determination kicks in?

Try the kick-off phrase "In the next year I am most determined to..." and see what comes up.

Examining what happens when our determination wanes, so that we can catch ourselves, is also a useful journaling exercise. By recognising and naming our excuses, we put ourselves in a better position to avoid making them, because our integrity baulks at slippery behaviour.

Try the inquiries: "How easily do I let myself off the hook?", "What excuses do I make?"

13. Disappointed

Disappointment results from attachment to high expectations which events or other people rarely fulfil. As disappointment festers it develops into a passive-aggressive simmering rage that is intuitively perceptible to others, and which is often referred to as an atmosphere or energy "hoover". To avoid being accused of this most unpleasant of social faux-pas it is better to cultivate an open, unattached optimism and acceptance in our daily life, and to express gratitude for whatever comes our way.

Once again this has rather an eastern philosophical feel from which we can glean many insights.

Disappointment fades away when we let go of the self-imposed obligation to meet our high expectations. This doesn't mean however that we should foster low expectations, but rather that we should always expect people are doing their best in the circumstances.

A useful inquiry to tackle disappointment is simply "What do I need to let go of?"

14. Dislocated

Ever feel like a fish out of water? Out of your depth? Itchy feet? Or that you're in the wrong place? Sometimes we can feel emotionally dislocated – when things don't seem to be going our way, or when we are experiencing a time where we don't seem to be getting what we want or need.

This isn't meant to sound petulant. Often we can feel off-key when our core values are being severely compromised. If being outdoors is important to you, getting fresh air, exercise or just simply admiring the natural world, you're going to react quite restlessly in circumstances that demand you stay indoors, with only the TV for company.

In order to understand why we feel like this, we need to become aware of what our core values are. What makes us smile? What makes us upset or angry?

An interesting journaling exercise here is to describe your perfect day. What activities, sights, sounds, smells feature in your ideal day? This can be as wild and wonderful as you like, though at first you might find that you feel confined to describing your perfect day in terms of what you currently know. It also serves us to be wary of trying too hard to be wild and wonderful, as if it's a competition. When we write in our journal there is no competition. There is no need to compromise our authenticity by coming up with the best ever perfect day scenario.

Once you begin to familiarise yourself with the kinds of things that would make your day perfect you will probably be surprised by how simple they can be. Small changes to our normal routine can make a huge difference to our outlook and our sense of well-being, as long as we make them authentically. Then we can overcome our feelings of dislocation and slot ourselves back into place.

15. Distressed

Our journal is typically the first port of call when we feel distressed. On these occasions it's good just to rant – to write whatever comes to the end of the pen, without a thought for niceties. This is when our journal serves us as an emotional safety valve, and why teenage diaries are so valuable during our most formative years.

Journaling doesn't necessarily eliminate the distressed feeling, but it does provide an outlet for us to express our emotions. It is also an opportunity for us to develop a new sense of perspective about what we are currently experiencing, and it helps in opening up a different channel of insight that often has the power to shift us to a new level of understanding about our situation, and what we can do to improve our experience.

16. Energetic

As a writer my experience of energy isn't always body-based. Sometimes there is a whole world of ideas jostling around in my head which makes life on the inside feel very energetic – even though on the outside I appear to be quite sedentary!

Using our journal to capture our ideas before they wither away can be very fulfilling. Ideas may turn into intentions, which may turn into plans and actions once they are out of our head and on the page. Alternatively they may just stay in idea form, and never hatch into anything more, but at least they gained expression and didn't stagnate in our mind, causing our energy levels to be unnecessarily sapped.

Writing makes me ravenous. Nervous energy eats up hundreds of calories and leaves me feeling hungry in a completely different way from physical activity. Becoming aware of our energy levels and being able to quantify them in some way is particularly useful if we're using our journal to keep track of certain physical symptoms.

Pick a period of time to check in with your energy levels, maybe over the course of a week or a month, to create your own energy scale, where 1 is the lowest score and ten is the highest. Get curious about what you notice at each level of the scale. How does your body feel? How motivated are you? What types of thoughts and ideas come to mind? How easy does it feel to get through your day?

17. Enthusiastic

Hooray – you've got an idea which you feel really enthusiastic about. It feels like such a perfect idea to you that you're almost scared to share it with anyone because they might pour cold water on it, or shoot it down in flames.

So don't. Pick up your journal and write it down. Elaborate on it. Enhance it. Develop it. Draw a picture. Make a project plan. Do whatever you need to do to build on your sense of enthusiasm. And beware of your inner critic. The moment you start to feel foolish, or the moment you start to come up with reasons why this idea won't work, you know your inner critic has popped up their head and decided to put in their twopenn'orth.

Enthusiasm is certainly an emotion to cultivate. So often we have our enthusiasm dampened by the judgements of others, but from this we need to learn not to stop being enthusiastic, but perhaps to be a bit more discerning about how we share our ideas.

Allow yourself to be enthusiastic, and write a letter to whoever owns the dissenting voice in your head explaining why they shall not succeed in raining on your parade this time.

18. Excited

Think back to your childhood and remember a time when you walked around school with a huge grin on your face because something was going to happen that you were so looking forwards to - ice cream for tea, a friend round to play, or a visit from Father Christmas.

What's your excited list? What are the things that make you smile on the inside whenever you look forward to them?

And if excitement is what you're feeling right now, get curious. What are you most excited by? What does it feel like? How is it making you think? What is your energy level like? What needs to happen next?

We can use our journals to capture our excitement, and once we notice it and name it, we can make it more accessible. Journal writing helps us to cultivate positive emotions in our lives, increasing our enthusiasm and energy for experiences that are authentically fulfilling.

19. Exhausted

It is well documented that our bodies often respond in paradoxical ways when experiencing certain extreme symptoms. Victims of hypothermia will begin to undress, increasing the rate of heat loss, while mental and physical exhaustion can result in insomnia as worries and anxieties magnify and prevent us from calming our minds for sleep.

Heightened self-awareness enables us to recognise the signs of our exhaustion. If we notice we're writing increasingly about our anxieties in our journal, and that these seem to be all-consuming, it's possible that we are suffering from over-tiredness and need to pay attention to getting some rest.

It is very tempting to keep writing, in the hope that we are getting it all out of our heads, but we must be vigilant against journaling becoming a vehicle for sleeplessness!

Be honest with yourself. Ask your body what it needs – and if it tells you it needs to sleep, grant it its wish.

20. Frustrated

What is it to be frustrated? Things aren't going to plan. Your travel arrangements have been disrupted. You didn't get the outcome you hoped for in your latest project. Your golf swing has gone to pot. Your partner wasn't in the mood at the same time as you.

Often our feelings of frustration arise because we expect things that aren't at all in our control to conform to what we want or need. The greater our need for control, the greater our frustration when things go wrong. So of course we can use our journals to rant about how annoying and useless and blameworthy is everything and everyone else in the world. This will get us so far in the self-expression stakes, but nowhere in our personal development.

Better to acknowledge the frustration and inquire into it. How does it feel? What are the tell-tale features of frustration that show up for us in our behaviour and our body? What are the familiar patterns that we notice about ourselves? And how does that feeling get in the way of what we actually want to achieve?

It also serves us to get curious about what degree of control we like to have over events and situations in our lives. What is your control-freakery score? What can you not be with?

The journal is the perfect place to engage in this frank and honest appraisal of our behavioural tendencies, and, if we are prepared to go so far, to find new answers for ourselves in the process of self-evaluation.

21. Guilty

When you're feeling guilty about something, be aware of the distinction between your perception of the situation and the reality. If the reality is that you did actually do something you oughtn't to have done, if you broke some rule or some law, or were wilfully neglectful or cruel, there is lots to ponder about and grow from.

Use your journal to inquire about where your actions have got you. What is the justification for what you did? What is the value you were trying to honour? Or what pain are you holding on to that causes you to inflict pain on others? How would you feel if someone did to you what you have done to them?

Again this is the kind of cross-examination that our human nature would have us shy away from. We all

116

have the capacity to go into denial, and to present endless self-justification as a way of resisting the judgments of others. It is hugely painful to have to face up to the fact that we have done wrong, not least because our culture is very much focussed on punishment rather than forgiveness and reconciliation.

Regardless of the religious connotations of forgiveness, and of the human reluctance to apologise authentically, saying sorry and asking for forgiveness are nevertheless important practices to develop. The more genuine we are in our apology, the quicker we and everyone around us can move on, without all the emotional baggage of guilt and resentment.

Inquiries to explore include:

- What must I forgive?
- How sincerely do I apologise?
- How sincerely do I accept apology?

However, if your guilty feeling arises more from your perception of what happened, or your concern about others' perceptions of you, then it is likely that you are being too hard on yourself. Raise your awareness of the real impact of your actions on others, and then take a more balanced view of your feelings.

22. Grateful

Using our journal to record our gratitude is one of the most enriching and enjoyable of all reflective writing practices. Immersing ourselves in the delicious things in our lives – our leisure, our friendships, the sensation of sun on our skin - provides a wealth of material for us to express gratitude for in writing. And remembering to be grateful when things don't quite go our way is also a useful way of re-setting our course and helping us get back on the right track. So when someone has wronged us, or when events haven't turned out the way we'd hoped, we can always look for the learning in the experience, and complete the kick-off:

"I'm grateful to x for..."

23. Grieving

There are few more abysmal human experiences than bereavement, and coming to terms with the loss of a loved one.

This is also a time when reflective writing can most serve us: to express our pain and anger, our gratitude for the one we've lost, and to make tentative steps towards finding any sort of new meaning or purpose for our own lives once again.

Allowing ourselves to free-write, without censoring any of our thoughts and emotions, can bring some comfort.

Contemplating the objects that our loved one held most dear, we might also write a tribute to them from the perspective of their favourite object. A pipe, a piano, a flat cap, a cherished toy – by giving these items a voice in our journal we can access an even deeper appreciation of the essence of their owner.

Allowing ourselves to chronicle our memories of the one we love, lists of their habits, physical characteristics, favourite catch phrases or TV programmes, and refer to them openly, can help.

Writing a letter to our loved one, and receiving their response, can bring us new insights and strength.

Death is something that emotionally we perhaps don't deal with very well in our western culture. People with religious faith have an in-built way of coming to terms with it; however for many non-religious people death represents a dreadful taboo. It is difficult to learn a different way to appreciate death in this context, which serves to distract us as far as possible from the reality of human experience.

The more we are open to the present moment, the more self-aware, and the more we nurture a sense of trust, confidence and resilience in our own consciousness and inner-strength, the more we will be able to equip ourselves with a perspective on the grieving process which allows us to embrace life once more.

24. Helpless

It is interesting to notice at what level of our consciousness we tend to feel helpless. For me, it is very much my logical, endlessly commentating and judging self which tends to run out of steam and feel helpless the most. As soon as I pick up my journal however I quickly and automatically invite a different level of my consciousness to the party, although so trapped have I been in my helplessness I often don't realise there is a different voice showing up until much later.

The trick is to notice and name the helpless feeling as soon as possible, then get curious about it. What physical and emotional symptoms accompany it? Often our logical brain wants to struggle on analysing and rationalising, finding something on which to blame our current state of mind. This is fine, and helpful to a degree, but journaling on the subject doesn't mean we need to perpetuate the struggle.

Our journal can help us build up our trust in our deeper faculties of consciousness, and realise the importance of certain human habits – such as sleep, exercise, sustenance and sex. Often when our mind is tired, it is our body that can show us the way. So we need to throw down our pen and surrender to our physical needs and resources.

Over time and over many journaling sessions which opened with the words "I feel so helpless and exhausted", I eventually learned to short-circuit the fight and just get some rest!

25. Hormonal

For many women using a journal to record their monthly symptoms, moods and thought patterns is a very useful way to understand the hormonal fluctuations their body goes through every cycle. For some women it is the only way to communicate to their health practitioner that they have a disruptive and serious enough problem that requires a more focussed intervention than just paracetamol and "having a word with themselves".

Some medical practitioners are beginning to acknowledge that paying attention to our menstrual and menopausal symptoms and becoming aware of their rhythms and idiosyncrasies for ourselves is sometimes sufficient in itself to improve our experience. By paying attention we somehow take control, feel less helpless and learn how to navigate through our symptoms in our own unique way. We also learn how our symptoms and hormonal levels can help rather than hinder us during our cycle. When oestrogen is rising at the beginning of our cycle we feel out-going and energetic, whereas in the second half of our cycle, when progesterone is on the rise, we become more introvert and unable to suffer fools.

With the benefit of our own insights into our cyclical modes and patterns we have greater opportunity to vary our own experiences according to how we are feeling, and to be more informed in our explanations about our behaviour! And of course this doesn't just apply to women. Men's hormonal cycles are much shorter – usually lasting 24 hours. It still may be useful for men to understand how they respond to different stimuli and circumstances depending on the time of the day.

26. Hostile

Think back to the last time you had to navigate traffic, either driving or cycling or on foot. How did you respond to your fellow travellers? How courteous were you? Or were you aware of feeling impatient about others' actions, even experiencing what has commonly become known as road rage?

And if you were to extend this inquiry into the rest of your life, how well do you receive ideas, suggestions and requests of others? How positively do you embrace new opportunities, or how quick are you to turn things and people away?

An underlying attitude of hostility to people and situations results in a highly negative life experience. And it's worth using your journal to get curious about what it is to be hostile. What is the mind chatter that gets in the way of a more positive attitude?

Being aware of the quality of our thinking, whether hostile or welcoming, is often enough for us to be able to choose a different state of mind. What happens in your body when you feel hostile? What facial expression are you displaying? What are you doing with your arms and hands? How does a feeling of hostility affect your neck, shoulders and back? If they feel tight and tense, it's probably not a good idea to pursue the line of thinking that is having this effect. So choose a different line of thinking, or pay attention to your body and take steps to reduce the physical tension.

If you are aware of a feeling of hostility what is it a sign of? For me, as soon as I sense a feeling of grumpiness I know that I probably need to rest, that sleeping is probably the best thing I could do.

Likewise, if you sense your hackles rising towards a particular person, perhaps the wisest course of action is to withdraw from their company. Your journal is always available for you to record what it is that is triggering your hostility. And notice how using it to document a diatribe of blame against another quickly becomes tiresome, and fails to resolve the feeling.

Try the inquiry "what is it about x that makes me feel so hostile?" Use your journal to identify as precisely as possible the things that push your buttons, This will raise your awareness and build your resilience in terms of how you might respond in the future.

27. Inspired

There are few feelings more delicious that being inspired. Suddenly there is clarity: an idea flows beautifully, and the right course of action emerges from what may previously have been a great deal of confusion or inaction.

Sometimes inspiration comes as you write. Sometimes inspiration, or lack of it, is why you write, or not. And other times you're riding such a wave of inspiration in your life generally that you don't have time to write. However it is always useful to have an inspirational resource in your journal in order to spur you on when times get tough and inspiration is in short supply.

Building an awareness of what inspires us is a useful practice. It's a bit like building gratitude or enthusiasm. It's an experience to cultivate consciously in our lives.

So you might make a deal with yourself to have an inspiration week or month, during which you will pay particular attention to all those people or happenings which inspire you. These things can be anything from the smallest gesture to the grandest project. It can be as humble as the girl on the check-out who went out of her way to help a customer in difficulty, to as awe-inspiring as Nelson Mandela or Mother Theresa.

Every single day things happen in our lives and in our awareness which can serve to inspire us. There is an art in making ourselves open to receive such inspiration and in getting curious about why certain actions and situations inspire us.

Try the kick-off phrases:

• "Today I was inspired by..."
• "The thing which most inspires me is..."
• "When I feel inspired I..."

These phrases enable us to reflect on our daily experience and our timeless values, and to build an awareness of how we behave and how our bodies feel when we are struck with inspiration.

28. Interested

What are you interested in? How does your interest manifest itself? What resources do you require to feed your interest? What opportunities do you use to deepen your interest?

Being interested in something – and following through with curiosity and practice – is an indicator of what type of person we are, what our strengths, skills, gifts and talents are. Our interests form an important set of distinctions that it serves us to be aware of in order to know ourselves.

A good journaling exercise is to take 10 minutes and write a list of 100 things that you're interested in. This could be a precursor to awakening your inspiration, or to helping you identify a new career or hobby.

Pay attention to those things which appear more than once on your list. What is it about these that captures your interest? What are these interests telling you about your current past-times or even your career?

And of course there is a different way to interpret the word interested. It can also apply to our more general state of mind than any specific set of activities or opportunities. An interested and curious state of mind however can lead to a more varied set of interests, and hence a wider set of choices.

Cultivate your interested state of mind by practising curiosity. Whenever you ask a question, make it a question which requires more than a yes/no answer. Practise asking open questions which invite more information. For example "What is it about x that is so interesting for me?" This is a much more curious and open-ended question than "why do I find x so interesting?"

As with so many feelings and emotions there is typically a physical posture which we can adopt to enhance our mood. How many times have we as children been told by our teachers to sit up, stop slouching and look smart? The whole idea is to reawaken our interest in whatever is being taught, or at least convey an impression that we are interested! However, what if you knew the particular physical posture that would help you transform your state of mind into one that is more interested in what is going on around you?

We often say "prick up your ears" to mean pay attention. Alternatively the "heads up" on something tends to be the real nugget of interest that it is most important to be aware of.

So maybe our teachers were right all along. Maybe consciously lifting our heads up can open up our minds to be more interested in what is going on around us.

Try the inquiry:

"What am I aware of when I lift up my head?"

29. Irritable

Much better to be able to pre-empt someone telling you how irritable you are today by admitting it first, than to be irritated even more by their observations and judgment.

You know what it's like. You know you're like a bear with a sore head, but it feels even worse when someone actually tells you that. It's much better to say "Leave me alone today - I'm like a bear with a sore head so best not to speak to me for a bit."

Not only does this spare us any further irritation it also demonstrates our self-awareness and our sense of perspective – and allows for even more to develop over the course of the day.

Our journal is a great place for us to develop a conscious awareness of what life is like for us when we're irritable. Irritability is not a mood to cultivate. It is an exhausting and unpleasant state of mind, but for many of us it is unavoidable at certain times.

Maybe we're tired, in need of food or exercise, sexually frustrated or just generally hormonal. There is any number of explanations for why irritability can sometimes get the better of us.

Sadly, without being aware of what it is that causes our irritability, we can unconsciously allow it to become our habitual state of mind, our default response. Over time this gives us the reputation and life experience of being quite hostile and negative, and begins to close down opportunities for us.

In our journals we can very quickly sum up what it is that is making us irritable:

"I am irritable because…"

If we find ourselves writing about our physical symptoms, then we can take a kinder perspective on ourselves, and perhaps finally give in to what our bodies are crying out for.

If we find ourselves writing about a disappointment we have experienced, or other set of circumstances which didn't turn out the way we wanted, then this provides a great opportunity for us to get curious about which of our values is being ignored, and what we need to do differently to make sure we honour the things that are important to us.

If we find ourselves beginning to blame others for our irritability we need to develop a different perspective. We need to take an empathetic glimpse at what life is like for that person. Perhaps use your journal to write a letter to them, and receive their response, or initiate a conversation with them and allow your sub-conscious mind to help you see things more from their perspective.

Alternatively you could skip straight to gratitude: "I am grateful to x for..."

30. Jittery

Jitteriness is the writer's enemy. It is distracting, and it stops us from being able to hold a pen or use a keyboard.

126

Everyone's experience and understanding of the jitters is different. It means different things to us all. Maybe it comes along with a sense of nervousness about an upcoming event. Maybe it is accompanied by butterflies. Maybe it's an indicator that we are afraid of what we must do to be successful, or even that we are afraid of success itself.

First of all, start with getting really clear about what you mean by feeling jittery. When does it happen? What triggers it? What does it feel like? How pleasant a feeling is it for you? When does it feel unpleasant?

Again, use your journal to help you determine whether having the jitters is an indicator of some physical need that you are not fulfilling. Maybe your blood sugar is too high or low. Ask your body what it needs when it feels the symptoms. You may not be able to write it down, but part of developing a reflective writing practice is to make self-reflection a more natural process – even if the writing bit doesn't happen.

It is intriguing to notice how accurately our body self-diagnoses, and how we can often identify our own cures for certain physical ailments, as long as we take the time to enquire of our body what it needs.

If however you know that jitteriness occurs ahead of something you must do in order to progress in life or work – maybe an audition, exam, sports match, presentation or important meeting – then find a way to embrace rather than resist the jitters.

Try the inquiries:

- What does it mean to be jittery?
- What do the jitters tell me?
- What can I do to dispel the jitters and succeed?
- How does being jittery enable me to succeed?

31. Joyful (Happy)

Our aim in life ought to be quite simple really – to enhance our experience of joyfulness. What would happen in the world if we all made a concerted effort to do things for joy and bring joy to others? Joyfulness has, I believe, a greater potential to be objectively and universally experienced than mere happiness. Being happy is highly subjective. What makes one person happy may be someone else's idea of hell. However, joyfulness is something than can be experienced in a crowd, or a congregation, or any gathering of people where there is a common focus, understanding and desire.

On a personal level, a joyful feeling is a much deeper, more visceral sense than happiness. Often when I feel joyful I cry, or I can't stop smiling or I have a strong feeling of elation somewhere in my core.

Joyfulness is definitely something to cultivate. And some of the most pleasurable journaling sessions happen when you feel a deeply quiet sense of joy.

So it's worthwhile getting curious. What triggers joyfulness for you? Perhaps it's being in nature, a particular piece of music, or having your loved ones around you.

It might be when you are engaged in an activity that you find most fulfilling or satisfying – kneading dough, painting, gardening, doing a jigsaw, journaling itself. Even the simplest activities that absorb us can bring us joy, because they enable us to focus on a task and stop the mind chatter, which is always trying to distract us with its self-importance.

Try the kick-off phrase "I am filled with joy when.." Alternatively, put on your favourite, most joy-inducing piece of music, and allow yourself to be fully transported. Then, take up your journal and free-write for five minutes. Marvel at how your joyfulness translates into written language!

32. Lazy

Laziness is an interesting concept. For some people it has extremely negative connotations, while others positively encourage it as a means to a happier and more stress-free lifestyle.

So it serves us to clarify what laziness means to us – and to identify how much of the laziness charge comes from others' judgements, or even that of our own inner critic.

Am I lazy if I don't do the gardening, the housework and the ironing? Possibly – it depends on what else I fill my time with. If I'm not doing my chores because I'm busy with work, and then when I'm not working I'm spending time having fun with my kids, then laziness would seem a cruel and inaccurate judgment on how I spend my time.

One man's sloth is another's productive effort. Like happiness, it is a highly subjective thing. What needs to be clear in our minds is whether we are judging ourselves by the right measure in determining how lazy or otherwise we are. If the amount we do or do not do is stressing us out then we need to take notice. However, if we can still remain effective and productive for relatively little effort, then surely that is to be applauded too.

And if it is the voice of our inner critic that we hear in our minds when we are questioning our level of laziness, then this is definitely something to disown.

Perhaps as a child we were labelled lazy, and have continued to carry this around with us, perhaps with severe consequences for our behaviour, either making us live up to the label or work ourselves into the ground to prove the accuser wrong.

Try the inquiry "how lazy/busy can I be – and still find life bearable?" Your journaling will help you find the right balance in this highly subjective matter.

33. Lonely

It is often said that you can never be lonely with a good book. Even if that book is your journal the same can be true. Gaining perspective on our life and becoming aware of the different levels of consciousness that are available to us can trick our mind into feeling less lonely. It can even start to feel positively crowded!

Striking up a dialogue in our journal with a comforting figure in our life, or even with our body or our creative self, is a way of accessing different voices which are meaningful to us, and which bring us different perspectives, as if from different people.

And sometimes we know that what's needed in order to help us feel more connected and less lonely in the world is to actually reach out and say hello, ask for help or do a favour for someone. The maxim 'give in order to receive' is a useful rule of thumb, and whenever we notice a lack of something in our life – like company, friendship or love - it's always worth reflecting on how much we are making ourselves available to others in those terms.

In order to alleviate feelings of loneliness try the inquiry "what more can I give", and act on what emerges for you.

34. Nervous

Being of a nervous disposition suggests an individual who is highly strung, chronically unable to relax, unduly worried and fearful, and perhaps dwelling on the least optimistic outcomes in life. And of course there can be acute nervousness in response to a particular event which can be extremely debilitating, even to the point of dictating whether the event goes ahead, or is ever repeated.

Using our journal we can swiftly identify the distinctions between chronic and acute nervousness and determine for ourselves which camp we fall into. And the fact is that developing a proper and authentic reflective writing practice can be the antidote for chronic nervousness as it enables us to appreciate our strengths and gifts much more keenly, as well as to help us identify unhelpful habits and behaviours. It also enables us to play with different thought patterns, and discover what the likely outcomes would be if we tried out different ways of viewing things.

Perhaps a way to approach nervousness is to begin to embrace it rather than resist it. Try the enquiries: What's good about being nervous? What does it demonstrate about me? How does it help?

Using our journal to change our pattern of behaviour to embrace rather than resist things in our experience often reveals surprising results. Our journal can become an emotional laboratory where we can test things out, learn more about our responses to things, and begin to shift our conditioned and habitual mental patterns.

35. Optimistic

So what of optimism? Looking on the bright side; expecting the best; seeing the silver lining; always accepting the present moment as just perfect.

Whether these attitudes are part of your everyday behaviour, whether they require a special effort, or whether they are just plain irritating, there is no denying that there is indeed benefit in looking for the good in every scenario, and not allowing ourselves to wallow too much in the doom and gloom.

Being optimistic is a lot about acceptance, and about learning. If we choose to look for what we can learn from a disappointing experience, then it can prove to be an important stepping stone for progress rather than a depressing excuse to give up.

Try the kick-off phrase "This is a perfect moment because…"

(Even using this at the least 'perfect moment' is a good practice to build up a sense of optimism.)

36. Overwhelmed

What is it to be overwhelmed? To have too much to do and not enough time; to always be putting on a brave face when it's the last thing you feel like doing; or to always try and take care of everything yourself, being seen to be strong in challenging circumstances when all you feel like doing is crawling away to hide.

We become overwhelmed when we've lost step with ourselves, and when we fail to communicate to others what our needs are. When it strikes it can be difficult to move beyond because we are invariably tired and emotional. Once again it is vital to recognise and respond to the signs our bodies are giving us – in my case usually tearfulness, exhaustion and irritability – and to follow through with what our body seems to be asking for.

Once we have gained some perspective and feel able to reflect on our experience, a useful next step is to get curious about what being overwhelmed means to us. Journaling on the following inquiries will help sharpen your awareness of this:

- What does it feel like to be overwhelmed?
- What overwhelms me?

My own experience of becoming overwhelmed is triggered by one or all of the "3 Ts" – tasks, tiredness and trying too hard. I experience it as rather a dizzy sensation, where I cannot keep still and cannot focus on one thing. No sooner do I attempt to deal with one thing, I immediately jump and try and deal with another. It triggers an awful restlessness and paralysing sense of obligation.

If the sense of being overwhelmed comes from too many tasks, write a list and begin to prioritise. If it comes from having too large a task to face, narrow your focus and start with a very small aspect or area, resolving not to worry about the rest until that bit is sorted.

If it's tiredness, ask your body what is needed. Pretty soon you'll be able to forego this step and find the way to simply take yourself off to bed, or to exercise – whatever works for you to overcome tiredness.

If it's a sense of trying to be something you're not, or taking on too much for yourself, get clear on who you can ask for help, or what requests you need to make to release you from the emotional overload of trying to be strong. A complaint is nothing more than a failed request. Those who manifest strong, unattractive tendencies towards burning flesh syndrome also tend to be life's major complainers and pessimists. If you're sensing this from someone, ask the question "How can I help?" or "What do you need?" in order for them to break their own cycle of feeling overwhelmed.

And if you're not accustomed to asking for help, journal on your own inquiry of what would help you in any given circumstance. Then go ahead and make your requests. People find these a lot easier to deal with than complaints.

37. Panicky

When the feeling of being overwhelmed escalates and takes over we can be flooded with a feeling of panic.

Writing is rarely possible in this state of mind. Our thoughts are jumpy and incoherent and our patience is non-existent. This is a place of zero objectivity. Our ability to look for a new perspective has temporarily left us and we are completely consumed by our fears.

Deep breaths are often recommended as an antidote to panic, and it certainly helps to consciously regulate our breathing to prevent hyper-ventilation. Another resource that is available to us in our body is our 'third eye' – the space on our forehead just above and between our eyes, which is an important component within meditative practices.

By leaning into this space and focusing our awareness on it we can begin to calm down.

Try this: sit on an upright chair with your back straight and feet placed squarely on the floor before you. Keeping your back straight, close your eyes and lean forwards from your waist. Place your elbow on your knee and gently press your third eye with your index finger. Keep all your attention focused on that spot.

As thoughts creep into your mind let them pass, stay focussed on the point between your eyebrows. This is a place of nothingness, allowing our mind to clear and our breath to fall naturally into its normal rhythm.

Maintain this position for as long as you can. Be aware of your stillness as you allow the mental panic to subside. Feel the relief as the panicky sensation dissipates, starved of your energy and attention.

Once your mind is clear you might now feel able to pick up your pen and reflect. Or you may experience a lightning flash of inspiration, the resolution to a problem that has seemed insoluble in the past. Once we clear space in our minds new solutions and possibilities are free to flood in.

38. Procrastinating (Avoiding)

Back at college we used to linger in the bar watching Neighbours after lunch or hang around in the porter's lodge just in case anybody were to deliver anything to our pigeon hole that needed urgent attention. All the while we were deftly avoiding the books and essays that awaited our attention.

These days this avoidance and procrastination still goes on, but it looks more like checking emails, snooping round Facebook or doing the next pile of laundry instead of getting on with anything more worthwhile.

In some ways journaling in itself can be a way of procrastinating. "I'll just write my journal" can become an excuse or something to hide behind instead of doing the work that really matters.

So journal-writers beware! Are you using your journal as a genuine tool to gain clarity and authentic direction, or is it a shield?

If ever you feel the paralysing pull of procrastination, and your pen is hovering desperately over your page in the hope something so profound will emerge to keep you there, shake yourself up with the following interjection:

"What the hell am I avoiding?"

Our journals are a great place for us to have a word with ourselves. What will the project you're avoiding mean to you? What will it bring you? How does it honestly compare to emails, Facebook or laundry?

Make a detailed note about what is the one single action you can take to progress your project the most in the shortest space of time right now. Then make a pact with yourself about how you will celebrate as soon as you've completed it.

39. Proud

Perhaps one of the reasons we have such a problem with self-esteem in our society is because of our entrenched cultural judgements about the emotion of pride.

Sometimes pride is considered a good thing, sometimes not. You can be accused of being too proud to accept help from someone, or you can be accused of not taking enough pride in your appearance. It's rather confusing.

Taking the positive perspective the feeling of pride that we are aiming for is a sense of high self-esteem, self-confidence, perhaps a feeling of belonging, or a feeling akin to love.

As always I would refer you to how it feels physically to experience this sense of pride. To have one's heart burst with pride is a common saying, and so it's interesting to notice whether this seems to be the area of the body that is affected for you when you experience a strong feeling of pride. Does your chest rise? Does it feel as if your ribs expand outwards? What is the physical feeling you get when you feel proud of yourself or of someone or something close to you?

To make a distinction with the opposite, more negative use of pride perhaps this would be more in line with a sense of stubbornness, or arrogance. It's interesting to reflect on how this type of pride would feel, and what we would be aware of within ourselves if we paused to analyse our sense of self once served with the accusation of this sort of pride. Physically where in your body do you experience stubbornness? It may be a sense of tension in your neck, shoulders or back.

Try inquiring into what it is you are resisting in order to unlock some of the stubborn feeling. Or try a conditional kick-off phrase such as "The worst thing that could happen if I allowed...would be..."

Alternatively commune with that part of your body where you are feeling the tension and ask it for its message.

40. Reflective

Building our reflective muscles is the main aim of journal writing, to raise our self- awareness and enable us to have a greater clarity of thought. There are a handful of very useful kick-off phrases and inquiries that can assist the reflective process, such as

- "It's been a time when..."
- "My intention is..."
- "I have learned..."
- "How do I distinguish...?"
- "Where am I heading?"
- "How does my body feel?"
- "What's the message for me in...?"

Becoming curious about our circumstances, our physical reality and our habits of thought is a useful practice in enabling us to be more reflective, and this in turn will help us to learn quicker and more authentically.

The more we practice being reflective, the more the mood will occur naturally for us. So sitting in a busy coffee shop with a delicious latte and our notebook, we can spend time getting curious, noticing our surroundings, what most catches our attention and how our environment makes us feel. This then becomes a journal entry which is not just a record of our momentary experience but also a snap-shot of a reflective process which is timeless, and which has the effect of seeming to expand time.

41. Relaxed

It's fun to write when you're feeling relaxed and just allow words to form at the end of the pen. There needs to be no hard thought, no reasoning, just an allowing, an unfolding of words and images onto the page.

Otherwise called free-writing, this can start anywhere and lead who knows where. It's a means of recording our day-dreams, and sometimes it gives us access to a sudden, unexpected flash of inspiration which we would probably miss if we weren't sitting with pen in hand.

Only a few seconds of writing is needed in this relaxed mode. As soon as we begin to observe what we're producing we engage a different, more analytical set of brainwaves and suddenly thought feels hard.

Take a deep breath. Close your eyes. Focus on the third eye, the space just above the mid-point of your brow, perhaps gently pressing there with your index finger. Allow your mind to clear. Then take up your pen and write the first words that occur to you. Continue to free-write for two minutes, allowing your pen to move across the page, allowing whatever words appear to form on the paper.

42. Resistant

What we resist persists. The longer we ignore something, fail to address an issue or simply refuse to countenance the truth of a situation, the worse things get, either materially and really, or in our minds. We become stuck in the same groove, making it increasingly likely that our circumstances will continue to reflect back to us the very thing that repulses us.

For example, failing to address a slow puncture in a tyre will guarantee that the tyre will never stop going flat, no matter how many times we attempt to fill it with air. Once we accept that the tyre is punctured, we can then take appropriate steps to repair it, and hence eradicate the persistent problem.

So when we continually experience the same issues over and over, we can reflect on what it is that we are not accepting about our circumstances or our attitude. What are we struggling against? What are we refusing to acknowledge?

This is closely related to the ideas of delusion and self-deception, and to stubbornness, the negative flipside of pride. A powerful inquiry to explore in your journal might be "What is the lie that I keep believing?"

43. Restless (Scattered)

It can be difficult to sit still long enough to write anything when we are struck by a feeling of restlessness. This can also feel like being somehow scattered, when our attention is being pulled in every direction and we feel like a cat on hot bricks, jumping from one thing to the next without much focus, and leaving a wake of unfinished things behind us.

This is when we can tend to feel most absent-minded and forgetful, losing keys, forgetting where we've put things and not knowing why we've gone into a particular room.

Paradoxically it would seem that this feeling arises not only when we're bored and lacking stimulating things to do, but also when we've a huge list of tasks to face, and we don't quite know where to start on it. In this respect restlessness is similar to procrastination and can be treated in a similar way, by biting hard on the bullet of "just doing it". What's needed is some focus, something for our restless mind to hone in on and get on with.

Dropping anchor for a while with our journal can be very helpful at times like this. Kick-off phrases to use in these circumstances might be:

- "The most urgent thing I have to do is…"
- "The most important thing I have to do is…"

Another clue to our restlessness and scattered feeling may be found in our immediate environment. If we're in quite a messy and disordered place, then it's likely that this physical reality will be reflected in our own state of mind, which can result in feelings of confusion and "cotton-wool brain".

Take a look around and make a note of the thing that is most catching your attention: a basket of ironing that needs to be done; papers scattered all over the desk; cluttered surfaces; toys and shoes all over the floor. Often we can spend our time ignoring these things in our rush to get on, but sometimes it's these very things that impede our progress, leaving us feeling restless and lacking in focus.

Creating a mind-map in our journal is also a useful technique to help us corral our wayward thoughts on a particular topic or project, enabling us to see the individual manageable chunks rather than be overwhelmed by everything at once. It can also reveal commonalities and connections between different elements and tasks which weren't obvious before, and which therefore help us find new ways forward.

44. Sad

What does it mean to be sad? What makes us sad? How do we know we're sad? How does sadness manifest for us?

When we're tempted to describe our mood as sad, is that the truth? Or has the term sadness become rather meaningless in its conventional usage? Is our emotion really something other than sadness – disappointment perhaps, grief or anger?

Writing a list of distinction, such as '100 things that make me sad', is a useful way of really getting to understand what drives this emotion in us. And of course, picking up our journal and capturing our sadness in the moment is also helpful. We can allow the eloquence of the emotion to come through and somehow contain it so that it doesn't overtake us.

The benefits of this are two-fold. Not only can we express ourselves cathartically, we can also glimpse insights into the things that are most important to us by understanding what it is that makes us sad.

My daughter feels sad when she sees an animal in imminent danger. My son is sad whenever he has to say goodbye to someone or something. I feel sad when there is neglect, or when an opportunity has been wasted. The thought of someone suffering alone makes me unutterably sad.

Using our journal to explore what makes us sad can serve us in bolstering our happiness and optimism. We can get clear on what triggers our emotion, and we can learn ways to maximise the moments in our lives when we are not sad.

In this way we can look for our own flipside of sadness, and strive for that rather than wallowing. Shedding a light on our sadness through our journals means that we can examine it more closely, study it objectively, learn from it and then move beyond it.

45. Scared

What's the difference between being scared and being afraid? Somehow being scared is more immediate, more physical and visceral, in response to a real object or phenomenon, while being afraid is perhaps more about our own cerebral constructs and interpretations.

We say things like "I'm scared of spiders or snakes or the dark or balloons going bang." Being scared of something has a child-like ring about it. But before we criticise our childishness, it's worth getting curious. Somehow being scared of a thing we know is real and outside of us feels more rational that being afraid of something that exists only in our imagination.

Distinguishing between two moods that seem very similar at first but which are actually quite different when we start to scrutinise them is a way of sharpening our thinking and becoming more aware of our habitual thought patterns.

A list of 100 things which scare you is likely to be different from 100 things you're afraid of. It's worth a play to see what emerges and to see what we learn. Perhaps it's a way of curing ourselves of our most irrational fears.

46. Strong

We talk about strength in physical, mental, and moral terms. We also speak of someone's strength of character. Are our bodies strong and healthy or weak and sickly? Do we have the mental discipline to pursue our dreams and goals? Are we blessed with a sense of moral integrity, and do we have the personal resilience to bounce back in adverse circumstances?

If you were to grade yourself in terms of how strong you were feeling today you might be referring to any one of these types of strength.

A kick-off phrase for the purposes of journaling on this mood might be

"I'm at my strongest when..." This in its turn might encourage us to think about our individual strengths, skills, talents, and things we're good at.

Another phrase is: "To be (physically/mentally/morally) strong is..."

And to deepen the inquiry further we can ask ourselves: "What do I gain from being strong?"

47. Stuck

Sometimes it's difficult to know when we're stuck. Because we're stuck! We can't see above or beyond our situation clearly enough to know that there is an alternative.

Being stuck means that we keep replaying habitual thought patterns and resigning ourselves to "the way things are", rather than getting curious about how things might be different. In some ways not being aware of our stuckness makes life easier. We just live the way we think we have to, accept the things we think we need to, and never ask any questions. Ignorance can be bliss!

However it's common to feel extremely restless and dissatisfied with the status quo. It's a natural part of human creativity and ingenuity to want to shift and change and go beyond circumstances that are causing us pain, difficulty or simply boredom. So when you begin to get a restless feeling, perhaps this is your body's way of telling you that you are stuck in your thinking, that there is more you can be doing, if only you change your outlook and thought patterns.

Bring to mind a particular situation, relationship or project that you feel stuck in. Try the following kick-off phrase:

- "My current attitude towards x is..."

Having reflected on your current perspective, challenge yourself to try different ways of looking at the situation. Find another six perspectives, beginning to write about each with the kick-off phrase:

- "Another way of looking at it is..."

Try the opposite perspective, the most challenging perspective, the scariest perspective, the perspective you could never do, the funniest perspective, the perspective your child or your grandmother would take.

Once you have a series of alternative perspectives you will already be starting to get a sense of becoming unstuck. Ideas will already have begun to flow, perhaps as early as the first word of your journal entry!

As I have said previously maintaining a reflective writing practice automatically grows us and makes us reach beyond the humdrum. The more reflective we allow ourselves to be, the more curious we become, and the more we come to rely on our inner authentic voice to guide us. This is how we gradually get unstuck.

48. Sympathetic

The definition of being sympathetic is having the capacity to be affected by the same emotion that someone else is feeling at the same time, and to be participating with another person in their difficulty. Sympathy is also what happens in nursery school when one child begins to cry, followed one by one by all the other children. It is also what happens in mob rule, when the anger and violence of one group affects others in the same way, escalating the risk of rioting.

The extension of this is being able to understand someone else's predicament in a much more sensitive and compassionate way and to empathise with them.

The distinction between sympathy and empathy is a subtle one, and it is not necessarily the case that one needs to feel sympathy before one can empathise.

It seems that empathy is a more objective experience, whereby we can appreciate someone else's emotion without necessarily sharing it. Empathy infers a healthy distance which helps keep things in perspective, whereas sympathy runs the risk of two people colluding over the same issue and approach, with neither moving forward nor learning anything new.

Reflective writing practice is fundamentally about growing and developing a more authentic and wise perspective. Being able to catch ourselves whenever there is collusion without the opportunity for growth is a huge benefit of deepening our self-awareness and being able to draw distinctions for ourselves in our behaviour and state of mind.

Try the inquiries:

- "How am I colluding?"
- "What is it to empathise?"
- "What does sympathy do?"

49. Upset

The difference between being upset and being sad is similar to the difference between being scared and being afraid. The first suggests a very real immediate response to a particular situation or set of circumstances, while the second suggests a more climatic background state of mind or outlook.

It's OK to be upset. Things upset us: they literally turn us on our heads and cause us to have a surprisingly topsy-turvy view of the world. It's a temporary inconvenience, one which we can recover from, perhaps with our own "self-righting mechanism", perhaps with little help from our friends.

When we're upset we tend to withdraw and feel sorry for ourselves in our pain and hurt. We run the risk of being consumed by our upset feeling, and naturally look to off load some of that overwhelming emotion by pointing the finger of blame elsewhere. However, this is always a costly misplacement of our focus and misuse of our energy. We fall into the trap of making an enormous mountain out of the tiniest tussock, and cause greater pain and hurt in the long run not only to ourselves but to others as well.

As long as the upset is a temporary upheaval rather than a constant feature of our state of mind and outlook, we have a great opportunity to view it objectively and get curious about it. Instead of dwelling on the discomfort of this and being compelled into blame of others, being upset affords us a fantastic opportunity to look at the world in a different way. Things are no longer as they first appeared to us. By looking at things from this startling topsy turvy perspective we have a golden opportunity to learn something new and develop a greater awareness of reality. Whenever an upsetting situation occurs, develop the habit of getting curious about this upended view of things. If a situation is no longer as it first appeared in what way is it different? What do you learn from the difference that is revealed?

50. Creative

Creativity is one of those words that sends people into a spin, either because they don't consider themselves to be creative (as in "I can't draw/write/make up stories/knit/sew/do craft"), or because they don't understand or value their creativity.

For me being creative is all about having ideas and acting on them, and making clever use of all the resources that are available in the moment.

One of my favourite challenges is coming up with a tasty family meal from limited ingredients. It's an opportunity to get creative in the kitchen and use up whatever's left in the larder. This is about applying ideas to the resources available and making something from them which is greater than the sum of its parts.

So let's clarify what creativity is in the context of our journal writing. Of course we can use our journals to draw, to paint, to write poetry or prose, to design things we're going to make, to dream up new business ideas, the layout for our brand new self-built home, or a new decorating scheme for the home we already have. A journal is not just about writing language in orderly lines. Anything can be included that helps us clarify our vision and make meaning out of our experience.

But being creative is not necessarily about creating something out of nowhere, out of our imagination; and it certainly isn't contingent upon how well we think we can express ourselves. Creativity is a constant feature of the human mind. Our thoughts are always trying to create something new, or find answers to questions that have bugged us for a while. Often we can simply pose ourselves a question and hold it in mind for a while, without thinking hard about it, and eventually, after a period of time, our ever creative thoughts will deliver the answer to us.

Writing a journal gives us the opportunity to listen to our thoughts, trust their wisdom and allow them to lead us where they will.

Try these kick-off phrases to begin thinking about your own creativity:

- "The resources available to me are…"
- "To be creative is to…"
- "My creative self is…"

Alternatively, write a letter to your creative self. Begin it "Dear Creative Self." What questions do you have of your creativity? What do you want your creative self to know? And what do you want your creative self to share with you?

Having written the letter, be still for a few minutes, then take up your pen and write the response. What does your creative self want you to know? What message does your creative self have for you? What guidance can your creativity give you?

Life Event Index

Use this reference guide to find journaling prompts and exercises that suit your current circumstances in life. Many of these exercises are repeated across different life events, demonstrating how adaptable they can be depending upon the lens through which they are viewed. Some may become favourites that you will return to again and again. Or you may be inspired to devise your own for different situations. Whatever works for you the important thing is that we raise our conscious awareness of our experience, and reflect on what our next steps could be.

Life Event	Chapters	Exercises
New beginnings *The start of a new "school" year; the time for resolutions; a new creative project or venture; starting a new job; moving house: all these things are examples of new beginnings. It can be a time of great energy and enthusiasm, and also a time of uncertainty. These exercises are to help explore our experience of these moments, and prepare to make the most of our new start.*	Weighing Anchor Setting the Course Safe Moorings	Kick-off (1) Back in time (4) Lists of distinction (5) Mix n' match (7) Letter from the future (8) Challenge (27)

Reaching a crossroads *The choices we make in our life dictate how successful or fulfilling our experience is going to be. Sometimes the choices we face feel like a fork in the road, and it can feel as if we are leaving behind a whole life that we've become very used to. This can be very scary, and can feel as if we no longer know who we are. Here are a few exercises to reinforce our personal resilience at challenging times.*	Foundering Discovering the Buried Treasure	Absolute truths (18) Hidden voices (21) Taking ownership (23) The golden thread of integrity (24)
Facing redundancy *The "r" word isn't quite as terrifying as it used to be; for some people it is just the nudge they need to dream up a new life for themselves. These exercises are for connecting us with what is real and true, and to beat off any negative thought patterns that might hold us back.*	Weighing Anchor Foundering Discovering the Buried Treasure Safe Moorings	Getting present (2) Absolute truths (18) Inner Critic (19) Job description (20) Ranting (22) Challenge (27)

Bereavement *When we lose the physical presence of a loved one we still have the memories of their own particular wisdom. These exercises may help us stay connected to that.*	Weighing Anchor Logging the Journey Foundering Safe Moorings	Writing as.. (3) Pen portrait (10) RSVP (17) Letter to… Writing about Writing in the third person Reframing (26)
Letting go of the past *Our past experience provides us with many stories about ourselves, not all of which are always helpful. These exercises are meant to help shift perspective and move on.*	Foundering Safe Moorings	Disentangling (16) RSVP (17) Absolute truths (18) Challenge (27)

Falling in love *A time to cherish if you can sit still for long enough! What is it about your love that you most appreciate? How does it make you feel? What will you remember forever?*	Logging the Journey Diving In	Sensory Survey (9) Pen portrait (10) Playing with metaphors (12) Thought movies (15)
Taking a break *Perfect for holiday-time journaling, helping us to immerse ourselves into our time-off and relish the sights, sounds and senses of our relaxation. A time to reconnect with our body, our intuition and our dreams.*	Logging the Journey Diving In Safe Moorings	Sensory Survey (9) Pen Portraits (10) Greet your body (13) Communing (14) Dream-logging Snapshots (25)
On the rebound *Any sort of rejection leaves us needing to make peace with the past and gird our loins for the future. It's a time for naming and shaming the gremlins, reminding ourselves of our own innate wisdom and throwing down some serious gauntlets at*	Setting the Course Foundering Discovering the Buried Treasure	Mix 'n' Match (7) Disentangling (16) RSVP (17) Inner critic (19) Hidden Voices (21)

our own feet.		Ranting (22)
		Taking ownership (23)
		The golden thread (24)
		Reframing (26)
	Safe Moorings	Challenge (27)
Becoming a leader	Setting the Course	Lists of Distinction (5)
With deeper self-awareness and greater appreciation of our own and others' strengths and vulnerabilities we become more confident, wise and able to lead. Whether at home, at work or in the community, don't be surprised if people begin to look to you for direction. Use these exercises to reflect on your role.		Values Inquiry (6)
		Mix n' match (7)
	Logging the Journey	A life in a day (11)
	Foundering	Job description (20)
	Safe Moorings	Taking ownership (23)
		Snapshots (25)
Looking for inspiration	Setting the Course	Back in time (4)
Do you need to be inspired to write? Or do you write to be inspired? Play with time, ask 'what if?' look outside, look inside, and pretend. See what inspiration	Logging the Journey	Mix n Match (7)
	Diving in	Pen portraits (10)
	Discovering the Buried Treasure	Playing with metaphors (12)

awaits you in these exercises.		Communing (14)
		The golden thread (24)
	Safe Moorings	Reframing (26)
Expecting a baby *New life is on its way and it's time to focus on your physical and emotional well-being. It's a time to set your intentions for the next generation, and give voice to your hopes and dreams.*	Logging the Journey Diving In	A life in a day (11) Greet your body (13) Communing (14) Dream-logging Letter to..
Getting married *Life is no longer going to be about one person. There's going to be an amazing celebration, and then the lifetime's work of compromise begins. Be prepared!*	Setting the Course Logging the Journey Discovering the Buried Treasure Safe Moorings	Values Inquiry (6) Letter from the future (8) A life in a day (11) Taking ownership (23) Snapshots (25)
Becoming a Grandparent *How will you approach your relationship with your grandchildren? A grandparent is*	Weighing Anchor Setting the Course Logging the Journey	Kick-off phrases (1) Lists of Distinction (5) Playing with

often the most influential person in a child's life: what kind of role model will you be, and how will you cherish the moments you spend together?	Safe Moorings	metaphors (12) Snapshots (25)

Tackling tricky relationships *Our journals don't necessarily show us how to be nice. They show us how to be authentic. Sometimes what we have to say won't go down well with others. For that we can always apologise. Rather these exercises help us find our own truth in the midst of others' trickiness.*	Foundering Discovering the Buried Treasure	Disentangling (16) RSVP (17) Absolute Truths (18) Ranting (22) Taking ownership (23)
Time for you *At one of my workshops Mae told me that in the midst of running a home and looking after her son who had been diagnosed with Asperger's Syndrome she was yearning for some "unadulterated me-time." Journaling led her to find her sense of identity, to be more creative, more able to handle difficult situations, and ultimately to take steps towards setting up her own business. Here are some exercises for you to indulge in your own me-time.*	Logging the Journey Diving in Discovering the Buried Treasure Safe Moorings	Sensory Survey (9) A life in a day (11) Greet your body (13) Thought movies (15) Hidden voices (21) The golden thread (24) Snapshots (25)

Getting promoted	Weighing Anchor	Writing as.. (3)
However you approach the idea of promotion, whether nervously or proudly, be clear about what you are bringing to the role, how you want to be, and what difference you will make. Have faith in your wisdom and don't be afraid to push yourself. These exercises may help you prepare.	Setting the Course Discovering the Buried Treasure Safe Moorings	Lists of Distinction (5) Letter from the future (8) The golden thread (24) Challenge (27)
Setting up your own business	Weighing Anchor	Writing as.. (3)
What floats your boat? What will fire you up every day? How can you be authentic in business? What's your main vulnerability – and how will you turn this into competitive edge? Use these exercises to find your answers.	Setting the Course Discovering the Buried Treasure Safe Moorings	Lists of Distinction (5) Letter from the future (8) Taking ownership (23) Challenge (27)

Exercise Index

Bibliography and Resources

Eat Pray Love by **Elizabeth Gilbert** – an interesting memoir demonstrating individual resilience and inner resourcefulness. Also made into a film – but the reflective passages of the book may not translate as well into cinema.

Thinking of Answers by **A.C. Grayling** – a tome which champions the philosophical and reflective activity of thinking for oneself about what it is we should be creating for our life out of our abilities, talents, interests, commitments and goals.

Blue Moon Diary **published by Susan Russell** www.susan-russell.com – a notebook that contains valuable information about the female cycle, with space to record symptoms and to reflect on events and emotions. The graphing pages are useful to see the ebb and flow of symptoms and moods over time.

www.myhormonesmademedoit.com – an entertaining and useful website by Gabrielle Lichterman, providing the 'Hormone Horoscope' and tips for managing ourselves, our mood and our life through our hormone cycles.

The Hero with a Thousand Faces by **Joseph Campbell** – seminal text exploring the theory that all mythology from around the world is founded in the same "hero's journey" structure.

Loving what is by **Byron Katie and Stephen Mitchell** – a very useful and insightful book that offers a template of questions to accompany reflective practice and help you get to the truth of every situation.

The Master and his Emissary by **Iain McGilchrist** – extremely well-researched examination of how culture is shaped by the features and characteristics of thought generated within the dominant hemisphere of the brain – typically the left-brain in the West.

I is an Other: The secret Life of metaphor and how it shapes the way we see the world by **James Geary** – an interesting insight into the importance of story and metaphorical narrative for us to make sense of experience and lead morally sound lives.

www.moodscope.com – an online tool enabling users to track their overall mood on a daily basis, see the ebb and flow of our moods, and even have the results of each day's mood test sent to trusted friends who can check on us if the test shows we're low.

www.ianwallacedreams.com – an informative site from psychologist and Radio 2's dream expert Ian Wallace, urging us to recognise our dreams as useful tools to help us interpret our reality and get to know who we are.

Medicine Cards by **Jamie Sams and David Carson** – a set of cards depicting animals familiar to Native American culture and an accompanying book which describes each animal's particular message and the different ways of using the cards.

Exercise is good for your waistline -- but it's a writing exercise. Association for Psychological Science (2012, January4) ScienceDaily.com article quoting and referring to: C. Logel, G. L. Cohen. **The Role of the Self in Physical Health: Testing the Effect of a Values-Affirmation Intervention on Weight Loss** *Psychological Science*, 2011

To find out more about UK-based journaling retreats, workshops and products, to share your ideas and insights, or simply to stay inspired on your journaling adventure, keep in touch on Facebook, at The Journal Writer's Handbook page, or by checking out my blog www.journalwritershandbook.co.uk.